WEATHER

AT SEA

Dedication: In memory of Nelson, Chief Forecasting Spaniel from 2007 to 2020, and the originator of the 'Spaniel Saturation Index' as a measure of puddle depth.

Other books in the series

A series of practical books for the cruising sailor

Visit **www.fernhurstbooks.com** to find out more...

SKIPPER'S LIBRARY

WEATHER
AT SEA

CRUISING SKIPPER'S GUIDE TO THE WEATHER

SIMON ROWELL

FERNHURST
BOOKS

Published in 2020 by Fernhurst Books Limited.

The Windmill, Mill Lane, Harbury, Leamington Spa, Warwickshire. CV33 9HP, UK

Tel: +44 (0) 1926 337488 | www.fernhurstbooks.com

A catalogue record for this book is available from the British Library
ISBN 9781912621088

Front cover photograph © Drozdin Vladimir / shutterstock.com
All photographs, diagrams, data and charts © Simon Rowell except as indicated on p94.

Designed by Daniel Stephen
Printed in Czech Republic by Finidr

CONTENTS

SIMON ROWELL
WORLD CLASS WEATHER FORECASTER

Simon Rowell started his working life as an engineer on oil rigs in various, usually insalubrious, parts of the world which gave him a thorough grasp of the many and varied uses of both gaffer and self-amalgamating tape.

He has been a yachting professional since 1997, starting off as an instructor before working for Clipper Ventures both as a round the world race skipper on the winning boat in the 2002 race and as assistant race director in charge of the day to day operations and all the skipper and crew training for the 2005 race.

He is an RYA Ocean Yachtmaster Examiner® and spent two years as Chief Instructor at UKSA in Cowes before going back to university in 2009 to study meteorology at the University of Reading, finishing the MSc course in 2010 with a distinction and a dissertation investigating aspects of how hurricanes start in the North Atlantic.

Simon has forecasted for clients of many descriptions – race-winning ocean rowers, private yachts, the Clipper Race since 2011, TV production companies, superyachts, expedition yachts, events such as the Round the Island Race, record-breaking swims, a Rugby World Cup team and keelboat regattas.

Since 2015 he has been the meteorologist for the British Sailing Team. He says, *"forecasting at the Olympics and Paralympics in Rio was fantastic, if rather challenging"*. Like the athletes, he looks forward to the challenges at the Tokyo Olympics if and when it happens.

He lives with his wife Gail in Cornwall on the eastern side of the Carrick Roads in Falmouth Harbour with their spaniel Molly.

FOREWORD

I first worked with Simon when, halfway through the 2000/01 Clipper Race, we were looking for a replacement skipper. He came on board in Singapore. We were impressed enough to employ him to help with the training for the 2002/03 race, but he was not intending to participate in the race itself. However, once again, he answered our call to be a replacement skipper, this time after just one leg. And he led his team around the world to victory. He was Assistant Race Director for the next race.

Once he got his Masters in meteorology, it was natural that we used Simon to provide weather information for the Clipper Race which he has done for five races so far. I have also used his weather forecasting services myself, both for races and for private voyages.

It was during the single-handed Route du Rhum in 2014 that he proudly informed me that one of my French competitors had a team of three weather forecasters working around the clock in 8-hour shifts, whereas I just had him and his two spaniels. I replied that the spaniels were OK at least! But Simon proved the better forecaster, giving me third in my class in this single-handed trans-Atlantic race.

But seriously, Simon has provided the Clipper Race, our skippers and crews and me guidance about the weather for nearly ten years now and I rely on it completely. In a sport that is reliant on natural forces, understanding those forces is fundamental to progress and safety. An understanding of the basics of meteorology is as fundamental to a sailor as knowing how to tie a bowline. Simon understands what a sailor needs to know and explains it from the sailor's point of view rather than from a meteorologist's perspective which is invaluable for the sailor out there on the oceans.

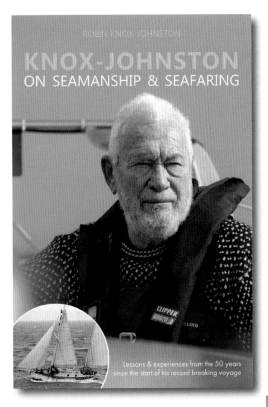

This book will allow you to benefit in the same way and I thoroughly recommend it to you.

Sir Robin Knox-Johnston
September 2020

INTRODUCTION

This book is set out to go through global, regional and then local weather patterns from a practical, on the water, sailor's point of view. The basic physics is explained simply, and the various phenomena are taken back as close to first principles as possible to try to keep a thread running from the large to the small. These are put in context with real situations to encourage the application of weather theory to practical sailing scenarios.

The way I've explained things comes from years of teaching weather courses to sailors, coaches and sailing instructors, and it is how I've come to understand how things work, so any liberties with the science are entirely of my own making.

It's quite easy to become competent at forecasting and using weather information – to get good at it, as with most things, requires practice. There's no better way of doing this than by looking at a forecast chart wherever you are once a day, whether you're on the water or not. If you try to relate that to what actually happens then, very soon, you will find that your forecasting skill and consistency get better. It's also a nice way to relax for a few minutes in the middle of a busy day.

I hope it's useful and enjoyable – any feedback is always gratefully received!

Simon Rowell
September 2020

UNITS USED

Pressure: Hectopascals (hPa) or millibars (mb). 1hPa = 1mb.

Wind speed: Knots (kts) or metres/second (m/s). 1kt = 1 nautical mile/hour = 1,852m/3,600s ≈ 0.5m/s.

Temperature: Degrees Celsius (°C).

Decametres: 10's of metres (dm). 564dm = 5,640m.

Geopotential metres (gpm): A scientific measurement that considers how gravity decreases as you move away from the Earth. For our purposes 1gpm = 1m. You'll see this sometimes on 500hPa charts.

1
GLOBAL WEATHER PATTERNS

Why do we have weather at all? What stops the atmosphere being a uniform blanket of air, sitting at rest over the Earth's surface?

The answer to both these questions is 'the Sun'.

The Sun provides a virtually constant supply of heat to the top of the atmosphere, in the form of ultra-violet (UV) radiation. This is called the 'solar constant', just under $1.4kW/m^2$, on average roughly half a boiling kettle's worth of power for every square metre. The 'on average' part of that is the key – because the Earth sits at an angle of 23° 26' to the orbital plane, the amount of energy actually received at a particular location on the surface depends on the latitude and the time of year.

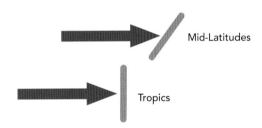

More energy hits the surface per square metre at the Equator than at the Poles

We live, work and sail in the lowest layer of the atmosphere, the troposphere, which is, on average, 16km deep (more at the Equator where it's warmer, less at the Poles where it's colder). Above that is the stratosphere, which goes up to around 50km and contains the ozone layer. Most of

Northern Hemisphere Summer

Southern Hemisphere Summer

The Earth's angle to the orbital plane gives us our seasons

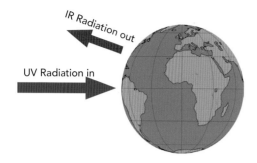

Ultra-violet radiation into the Earth's surface, infra-red out

the dangerous components of the Sun's UV radiation are absorbed by the ozone layer. Due to the different chemical composition of the troposphere, the remaining UV light is not absorbed there and so it passes through the troposphere to be absorbed by the Earth's surface, be it water or land. This in turn warms the surface which re-radiates energy back into the troposphere from below. Because this is so much cooler

than the Sun, the wavelength is longer – it is infra-red (IR) – and so the troposphere is heated from below even though the ultimate source of all this energy is the Sun above.

This heating from below is the source of the convection that we're familiar with – thermals rising up from hotter patches of ground for birds and gliders to use, for example.

This basic view, when combined with the surface differences due to land masses, deserts, seas, ice caps, etc., gives the following global surface temperature distributions for June to August (Northern Hemisphere summer) and December to February (Northern Hemisphere winter). An important point to note is that while the temperature changes dramatically at the Poles, it doesn't really do so at the Equator – the warm band just moves north or south with the Sun.

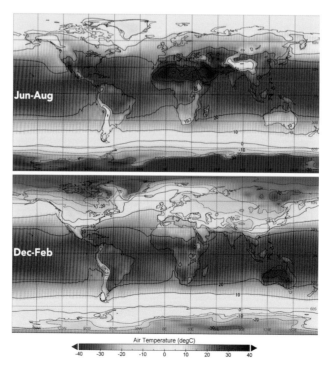

Surface temperature averages (°C) for Jun-Aug (top), and Dec-Feb (bottom) showing how the greatest temperature difference with the seasons is at the Poles while the Tropics change slightly

THE EFFECT OF SURFACE TEMPERATURE DIFFERENCES – THERMAL WIND

Think of a theoretical vertical section of the atmosphere, with the surface at the same temperature everywhere and a surface pressure of 1,000hPa. As you get higher the pressure will decrease uniformly, so that any given height the pressure is the same.

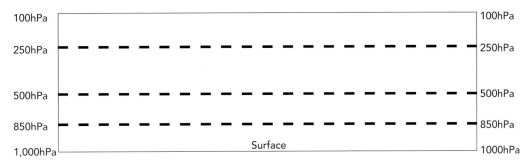

A theoretical vertical section of the atmosphere with the surface at the same temperature with the pressure decreasing uniformly as you get higher (the lines of equal pressure are black, and the height is indicated by horizontal white dashed lines; they overlay here as the surface temperature is uniform)

Now let us consider what happens if the surface on the left-hand side is heated:

1. If the left-hand side of the surface is heated (say by having more solar heat per square metre in the Tropics) then, as it gets hotter, the air above it expands. Now at any given height on the left, the pressure is more than the same height on the right, above the cold part (say at the Poles). Looking at the top dashed white height line the pressure above the hot surface is around 350hPa while above the cold surface on the right it's still 100hPa.

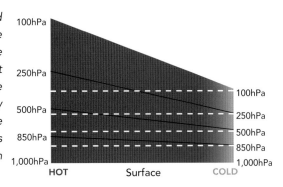

2. This pressure imbalance causes wind to blow from above the warm surface to above the cold surface. As this means that air is physically removed from above the warm bit, the surface pressure there decreases, while the air arriving above the cold bit causes the surface pressure there to increase.

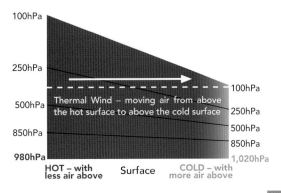

3. *This surface pressure difference causes a surface wind to flow from the high pressure at the cold surface towards the low pressure at the warm one – and now we have a thermal wind circulation.*

You can apply this thermal wind circulation to all sorts of scales:

- From global with the Trade Winds
- To local with sea breeze

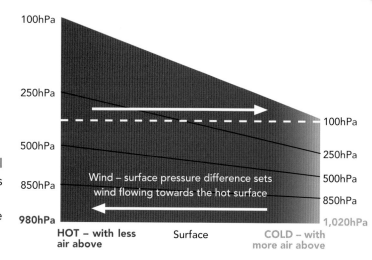

What this would imply is that we should get reasonably constant wind going from the Poles to the Equator on the surface, and the other way round at the top of the troposphere. However, so far, we've ignored the relatively minor details that the Earth is not flat and is also rotating.

THE CORIOLIS EFFECT

Before we get into the Coriolis Effect itself, think of the atmosphere as being made up of discrete parcels of air which get moved around and expand and contract as per the laws of physics. This is a pretty good approximation to what actually happens – if you look at steam coming from a power station chimney, for example, it doesn't immediately disperse but will stay in a reasonably organised column for a while.

This will help understand what happens to the air.

The Coriolis Effect occurs because the Earth is both spherical and rotating to the east. This means that the eastwards speed of any part of the Earth's surface depends on how far away from the Equator it is:

- At the Equator the ground moves eastwards at 21,600 miles every 24 hours, i.e. at 900 knots

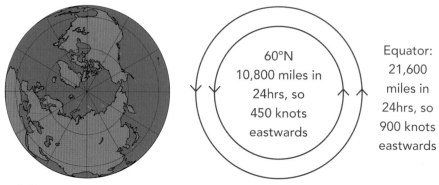

Viewing the Earth from above the North Pole: the differing east-going speeds of the Earth's surface at different latitudes

- At 60°N or S it is only 10,800 miles every 24 hours, i.e. at 450 knots
- At the Poles the ground doesn't move eastwards at all

This means that, if there is no wind, the air parcels above the Earth are also moving eastwards at the same speed as the surface beneath them (like the steam from the chimney).

To explain what the Coriolis Effect does, imagine that you are standing on the Equator looking north at an oak tree, with a line of horticulturally unlikely trees on your left at regular intervals.

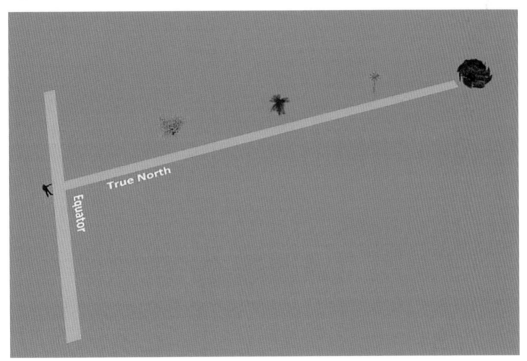

The scenario as seen from above: standing on the Equator looking at the oak tree directly north

The view looking north from the Equator (bottom) with a cherry blossom tree, a date palm, a coconut tree and finally an oak tree furthest (and directly) north

Imagine there is a gentle southerly breeze blowing and you then release a balloon at the Equator:

1. When you release the balloon at the Equator, it will have the 900 knots of speed to the east as on the surface as explained on p12, and it will maintain this as it is blown north by the gentle southerly breeze.

2. The pink cherry tree, however, will have less eastward speed than this as it's not on the Equator, and so, by the time the balloon gets there, it will have moved to the right with respect to the cherry tree.

3. The effect is increased by the time the balloon gets as far north as the low date palm which is going slower to the east than the cherry tree as it is further from the Equator.

4. This movement to the right is further increased by the same reasoning past the tall coconut palm.

5. And even more when it is as far north as the oak tree.

The effect is exaggerated in this example, but it is what happens in reality, and the motion of the balloon represents the motion of the air parcels around it.

This shows the Coriolis Effect – in the Northern Hemisphere it moves wind (and currents) to the right of their path, and in the Southern Hemisphere to the left. The effect increases with increasing latitude and with increasing wind speed.

It works whatever the initial direction of movement.

Try this – imagine a parcel of air coming due south at the oak tree. By the time it gets to the Equator it will have moved to its right.

THE JET STREAM

So, what does all this Coriolis Effect stuff do?

Let's think about two parcels of air in the upper part of the troposphere at around 200hPa above the Equator, i.e. above the hot part. There's a pressure differential pushing them away from above the Equator towards above the Poles, the cold surface areas (as explained on p12). One parcel goes south, the other north.

This is how the Jet Streams are formed, with an east-going upper air flow in both hemispheres. (This explanation does ignore several other physical forces but is still valid.)

Also, thinking back to thermal wind balance (p12), the greater the temperature difference, the stronger the wind is. This means that we'd expect stronger Jet Stream winds in winter when the difference between the surface temperatures at the Equator and the Poles is maximum. The chart overleaf shows this in the long term mean winds at 200hPa.

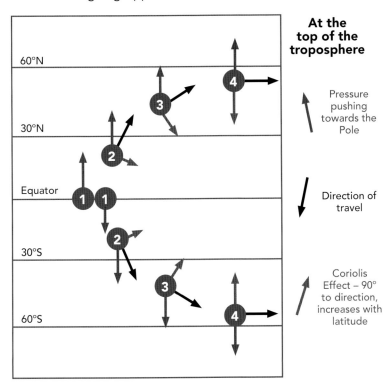

At the top of the troposphere

Pressure pushing towards the Pole

Direction of travel

Coriolis Effect – 90° to direction, increases with latitude

1. The parcels are above the Equator with no Coriolis Effect.

2. As the latitude increases so does Coriolis, at 90° to the direction of travel (right in the north, left in the south).

3. The Coriolis Effect increases with increasing latitude.

4. Eventually it balances the pressure pulling the air parcel towards the Pole, and the parcel travels east in equilibrium.

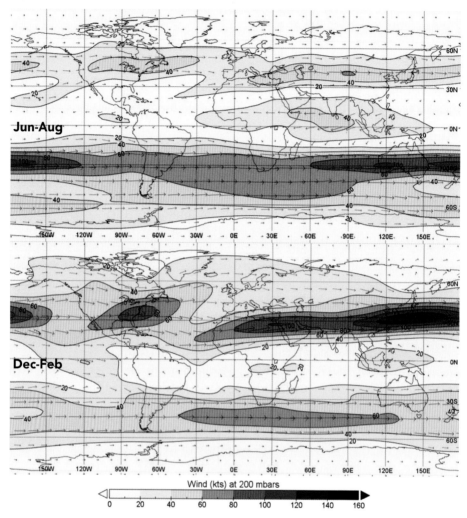

Wind (kts) at 200 mbars

Global upper level winds at 200hPa for Jun-Aug (top), Dec-Feb (bottom): the upper one is Northern Hemisphere summer, so the Southern Jet Stream is stronger, & vice-versa for the bottom

The shape of the Jet Streams in the two hemispheres are very different. The southern Jet Stream is much more uniform than the northern, and this is due to the very different land mass and therefore surface temperature distribution north and south of the Equator.

The Jet Stream is more than just a flat river of air at altitude. Taking the example of 120°E (which goes from the South Pole, over Antarctica, across Western Australia, then through Indonesia and the Philippines, up the east coast of China, across Siberia,

through the Arctic to the North Pole), the average wind speeds throughout this slice of the atmosphere in January, so Northern Hemisphere winter, are shown opposite.

This shows a South Pole to North Pole cross section from the surface at 1,000hPa to the top of the troposphere. The wind speeds are given in m/s, so the red zone centred at 200hPa at about 30°N shows 60m/s, or around 120kts, as a jet of wind coming out of the page towards you. This jet is deep too – going from 100hPa all the way down to around 700hPa.

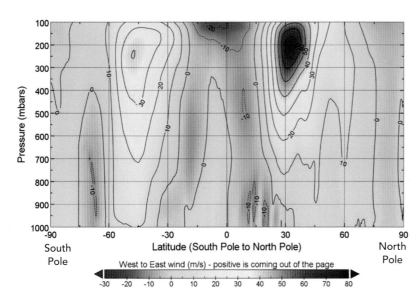

A vertical cross section showing wind speed (m/s) from Pole to Pole at 120°E for January 1968-1996

because it gives a good idea of where the low pressure systems are going. In general the centres of the surface low pressures move about 2-5° on the polewards side of the Jet Streams (so north of it in the Northern Hemisphere, south of it in the Southern). As the Jet Streams are much further above the more chaotic and difficult to forecast surface layers, the Jet Stream forecast for 5 to 7 days out is usually of reasonably good quality, so can give you a good idea of the general movement of weather systems that far ahead – you can't get a spot forecast, but you can tell whether your weather is going to be low or high pressure driven.

There are Jet Streams both sides of the Equator, but the winter one (Northern Hemisphere in this case) is strongest. The strongest part of the Jet Stream is at about 200hPa but is still present at about the same location at 500hPa, and this is why the 500hPa charts are very handy to locate the Jet Stream, as we will see later (p50).

The Jet Stream is useful for sailors

THE OCEAN HIGH PRESSURE SYSTEMS & HADLEY CELLS

We are familiar with weather forecasters talking about 'the North Atlantic high', or 'the Southern Indian Ocean high', and there are similar highs in all the major oceans at about 30° to 40° north and south of the Equator. These are large and generally fairly stable areas of higher mean sea level pressure. The idea of a polar high makes sense as the global thermal circulation ends up moving air to above the Poles (as we described when talking about the thermal wind circulation, see p12), but

that's not the case here.

As with most things meteorological, it comes down to the way the Sun heats the Earth's surface, and then how that heat, re-radiating back out from the surface as infra-red radiation, is distributed through the atmosphere. The diagram overleaf shows the same pole-to-pole vertical slice through the atmosphere at 120°E that we saw above, but now it shows the average temperature of the atmosphere for January 1968-1996.

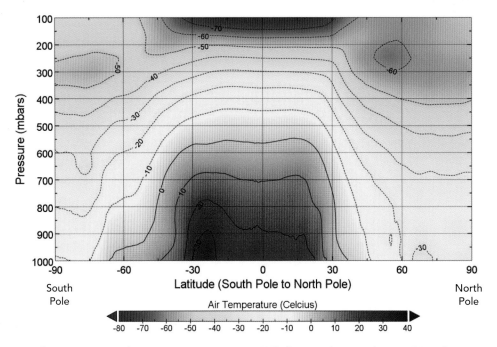

A vertical cross section showing air temperature (°C) from Pole to Pole at 120°E for January 1968-1996.

This is Northern Hemisphere winter, so the North Pole is very cold. Going south of the Equator there is a bubble of hotter air at 20-28°S extending up to about 800hPa – this is the air above the Western Australian Desert. However, above that the feature to note is that from about 30°S to 30°N the air at any given altitude is the same temperature, before dropping off either side of that. This occurs because the surface underneath here is heated strongly by the Sun and so in turn re-radiates enough heat to keep the air at a consistent temperature at any given altitude.

Either side of that, the heat coming up from the surface decreases, as discussed on p9, which means that air higher up cools down faster. This causes the cooling air to become less buoyant, so it starts to subside – this is what causes the mid-ocean high pressure systems. This large circulation, generally immediately north and south of the Equator, is known as the Hadley Cell, and it is strongest in the winter hemisphere. This is why we have stronger Trade Winds in winter.

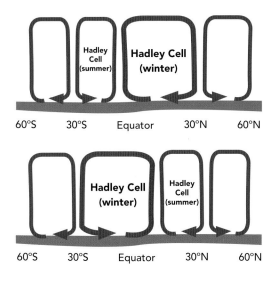

The Hadley Cell in winter for the Northern (top) and Southern (bottom) Hemispheres

On a global scale, the atmosphere is split into four main layers (see below). The part that humanity mostly inhabits is the lower one, the troposphere, which is anywhere from about 16km deep at the Equator where the surface is hottest to about 8km deep at the Poles. Above that is the stratosphere, with a transition zone, the tropopause.

Due to the chemical composition of the troposphere it doesn't absorb much short-wave radiation from the Sun, so it's heated from the surface (p9) and the temperature decreases with altitude. The stratosphere above it, however, absorbs short-wave radiation and so its temperature increases with altitude.

This means that any air parcels rising through the troposphere (for example near the Equator) will get to the top of the troposphere and then no longer be able to rise any further as the air above them is warmer. This is why the air at the top of the Hadley Cells cannot just keep rising. This is called a temperature inversion, and we'll see it again on a smaller scale when we discuss local effects.

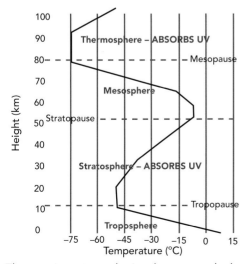

The main atmospheric layers and how temperature changes showing how the layers that absorb UV get warmer with altitude

HIGH PRESSURE SYSTEMS

The air comes into a high at the upper levels, descends, and then rotates out at the surface – clockwise in the Northern Hemisphere, anticlockwise in the Southern Hemisphere (because the Coriolis Effect works in the opposite direction in each).

Highs are more stable than low pressure systems and can stay in the same general area for days or more. The descending air started off around the Equator as the warmest part of the Hadley Cell circulation, and as it gets lower again the increasing pressure will cause it to heat up gradually, trying to get back to the same warm temperature it initially was. This is the same effect as your bicycle pump getting hot as you compress the air inside it.

Below this gradually warming descending air, the surface is heated by the Sun as there are no upper level clouds in the way, and this causes the lowest part of the troposphere to rise – we have convection. The descending air is often a little warmer than the air coming up from the surface as it started off at the Equator at a higher temperature, so where they meet the rising air is effectively capped by the warmer air above it – cooler air is less buoyant. This is another inversion, lower down than the one at the tropopause. We often see a broken thin layer of stratus here, and in the Tropics this is where we get Trade Wind cumulus clouds.

Because the air beneath this inversion is effectively trapped with convection continually lifting up from the surface this layer is often quite dusty over land or hazy over sea.

During the winter the surface heating is less than in the summer, so the days are characterised by beautifully clear skies and often bitingly low temperatures at night as there is no cloud cover to keep what little heat there is in.

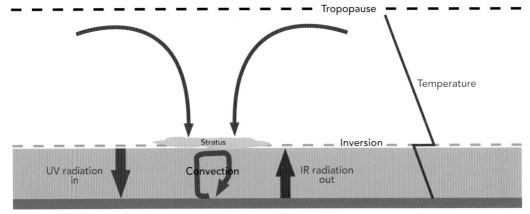

An inversion forming under a high pressure system

GLOBAL SURFACE PRESSURE DISTRIBUTION

Due to the increased temperature difference between the Equator and the winter Pole, the Hadley Cell is strongest in winter, which is when the steadiest and strongest Trade Winds blow.

Due to the Earth's rotation, and therefore the Coriolis Effect, the surface winds – the Trades – coming back from the surface high towards the Equator in the Northern Hemisphere do not blow from the north, but from the north-east, veering to the east the further west you go, and these give the ideal winds to travel from Europe across the Atlantic. The same thing happens in mirror image in the Southern Hemisphere, with the Southeast

Trades making the trip from Cape Town to Salvador in Brazil mostly a downwind romp.

The actual global surface pressure average is complicated by land masses, and the effect of the globally continuous Southern Ocean is very visible, giving a relatively low average pressure band encircling the Southern Hemisphere just north of Antarctica.

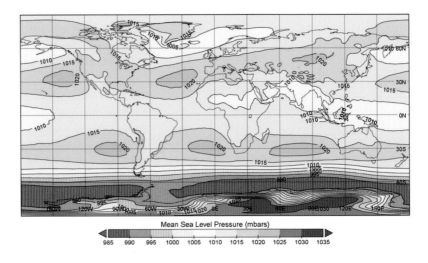

Annual average of sea level pressure 1948-2010 showing high pressures as blue, low pressures as red: the mid-ocean highs are clearly seen, as is the consistent track of low pressure systems around the Southern Ocean

2

WEATHER CHARTS, FORECAST TYPES, GRIB DATA & TERMINOLOGY

This section introduces the types of forecasts available and the terminology involved. This will then be used to explain the various weather phenomena that are regularly experienced. Detailed explanations of all the features will follow on through the book.

SYNOPTIC CHARTS

Synoptic charts are a generic name given to large scale weather maps showing areas of oceanic or continental scale, e.g. the synoptic chart for the region around Australia and New Zealand. Timewise there are two main types: analysis and forecast charts. Analysis charts show historical data up to the present, whereas forecast charts – well, they look ahead into the future. As for the information displayed, that can be of many different properties, from atmospheric pressure and precipitation to wind speed and direction and many more. The immediate ones we look at are surface pressure charts and upper atmosphere height charts.

SURFACE PRESSURE CHARTS

These show pressure reduced to mean sea level and have several specific features (see below). Different forecasting organisations have different presentations, but the basic information will be very similar. The surface chart is the only one where pressure is given at a particular height, in this case mean sea level, and while at sea this presents no problem as your ship's barometer is at sea level, if you sail inland at any altitude (or even below mean sea level if you're lucky enough to be in the Dead Sea) the pressure you read will not be the same as the surface chart due to the altitude difference. As we are particularly interested in the weather at the surface, the surface chart is the most direct source of information for our immediate weather information needs.

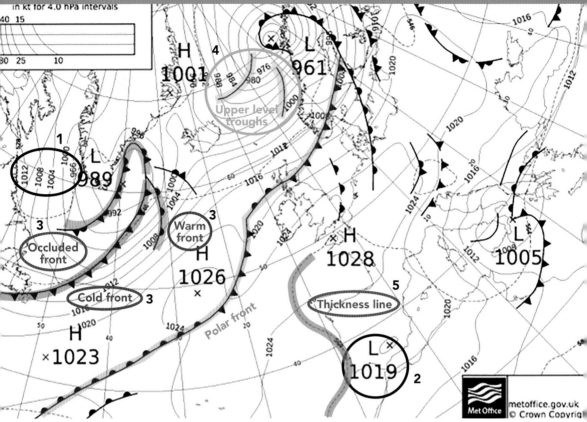

Met Office mean sea level forecast chart (contains public sector information licensed under the Open Government Licence v1.0)

Elements which feature in these charts are:

- **Isobars (1)**: Lines of equal surface pressure, with the pressure given in millibars (mb) or hectoPascals (hPa). These describe the shape of the pressure systems very much like contours on a land map.

- **Centres of rotation (2)**: Denoted by H for a high pressure, L for a low, these are the centres of a rotating synoptic system. Lows rotate anti-clockwise in the Northern Hemisphere, clockwise in the Southern, and vice-versa for highs. Some agencies, as shown here, put an X at the centre of rotation.

- **Cold, Warm & Occluded Fronts (3)**: Lines along which different air masses meet, and the source of much of our actual 'weather', i.e. rain, cloud, snow,

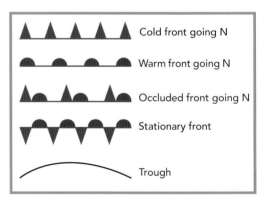

etc. Also shown are remnants of old fronts.

- **Troughs (4)**: These are an upper level feature often shown on surface charts. There will often be a line of rain in and ahead of the trough.

- **Thickness Lines (5)**: A bit more esoteric, showing the difference in height between the 1,000hPa and 500hPa heights – useful for working out whether rain, sleet or snow is on the way. Usually labelled as decametres (tens of metres).

Not all forecast agencies have the same format or data content – but they all have the advantage of being inspected and issued by a human forecaster after the numerical model has spat out the numbers.

UPPER LEVEL CHARTS

Unlike surface charts, which give the pressure at a single height, albeit mean sea level, upper level charts give the height at which a particular pressure is found. These heights are usually given in metres or decametres (tens of metres, dm) and are actually calculated as geopotential metres – for all practical purposes these can be thought of as metres. These height contours are just like the height contours on a land map and are used to look at the

shape of the atmosphere at various different pressure levels (see below). They are also directly related to the overall temperature of the atmosphere at any given time – the higher the height of any given pressure, the warmer, more expanded and therefore less dense is the atmosphere beneath it.

This map also features wind barbs.

Wind Barbs: usually given wind speed units, knots or m/s. A small barb is 5, a large one 10 & a triangle 50.

They refer to the location at the point end of the barb, and the wind is in the direction from which it comes.

If the chart is in knots, this barb would indicate 65kts from the NW.

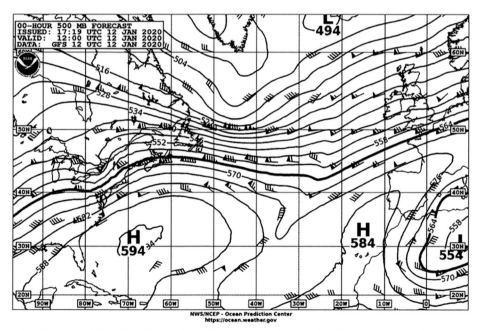

Upper level chart: 500hPa heights and wind barbs over the North Atlantic Ocean in decametres, 12 January 2020; the 564dm contour (thicker) is a good proxy for the centre of the Jet Stream

GRIB DATA

Organisations around the world invest massive amounts of time and money into the knowledge and computing power necessary to run weather prediction programs and, as we all know, the results of these are subject to occasional significant errors.

The forecasts that we are used to seeing are known as deterministic forecasts, which means that the computer model is set up with a set of initial conditions, and then allowed to run for whatever the forecast period is. These initial conditions are set at every corner of a 3D grid used to divide up the atmosphere and the oceans (see below) and the data sets produced are huge – the Met Office Unified Model at the time of writing has 70 atmospheric levels going up to 80km and 10km grid squares in its global model. Over the UK the resolution comes down to 1.5km squares.

The data that is produced is often in the form of GRIdded Binary data, known as GRIB files (.grb files). Some agencies' files are available freely off the web (search for GRIB data) and you can download the entire 3D model of the atmosphere if you have the

bandwidth and the storage space.

All PC-based navigation programs can read GRIB data, allowing you to overlay weather directly on to your digital chart, and there are many freely available GRIB viewers available.

At each corner of the grid the numerical weather program (NWP) calculates six properties – wind in three dimensions, humidity, temperature and pressure. Everything else comes from these, and properties such as cloud cover, rain and visibility are obtained by a process called parameterisation which works as follows: taking rainfall as an example, the program looks at the conditions at each corner of the box and assigns rainfall to occur at the more humid end of the box.

The box size also determines what

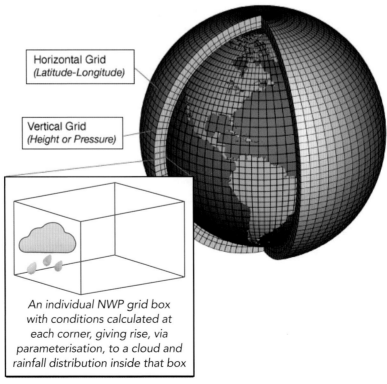

Horizontal Grid
(Latitude-Longitude)

Vertical Grid
(Height or Pressure)

An individual NWP grid box with conditions calculated at each corner, giving rise, via parameterisation, to a cloud and rainfall distribution inside that box

Splitting the atmosphere and the ocean into a 3D grid

size of weather feature can be picked up just by the model. For something to be picked out as a distinctive feature (say a low pressure system) it needs to be about 4 grid boxes wide, otherwise it just comes up as a blip. This means that if we take the UK Met Office global model, with 10km resolution, then the smallest feature that can be picked up is 40km across. That's a large squall cluster! Even its UK model with 1.5km spacing can only model features that are 6km across.

ENSEMBLE FORECASTS

Our usual weather forecast doesn't take into account any potential variations in initial conditions – these are checked as thoroughly as possible, but measurement and reporting errors do creep in. A modern technique which depends on massive computing power is that of ensemble forecasting, which takes the initial conditions, changes them slightly, runs the forecast, and then does that for many slightly different initial conditions. Each of these forecasts (known as an ensemble member) will develop independently, and their outputs tend to diverge as time goes on – as illustrated below – which shows 20 different ensemble forecasts, first at a 6-hour forecast time (very little divergence between each forecast) and then at 168-hours (1 week) where the spread is much greater.

This is very useful as it gives an idea of the probability of something happening. Taking the wind speed at 168 hours from the example below, a probability map of the wind being greater than 20kts is generated (see overleaf). If 12 of the 20 members show a wind speed greater than 20kts then the probability is 12/20, or 60%. This is shown just south east of Japan in this example.

It must be emphasised that this is still just a probability. Mother Nature does have a habit of laughing in the face of statistics, but it is still a very good way to get a feeling for how likely the forecast is to actually happen. If you have a high level of confidence, then that's good. Conversely, if the forecasts spread widely and there's no overall trend, that is also very useful to know.

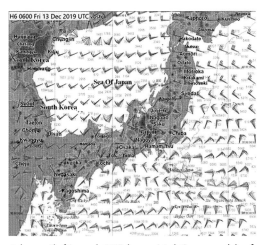
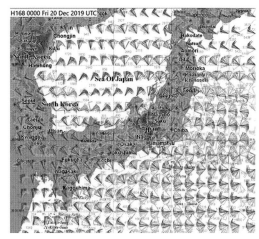

6-hour (left) and 168-hour (right) ensemble forecasts showing the wind barbs for 20 different ensemble members overlaid; the 6-hour forecast shows very little divergence, there's much more in the 168-hour forecast

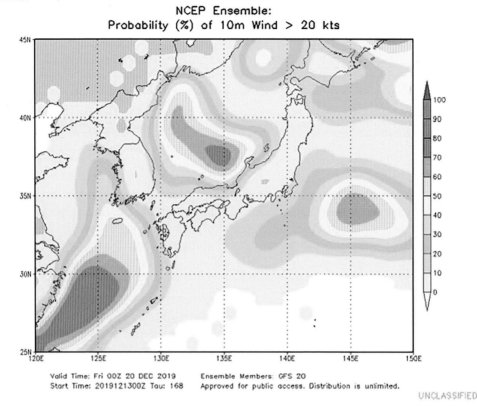

UNCLASSIFIED

NCEP Ensemble:
Probability (%) of 10m Wind > 20 kts

Valid Time: Fri 00Z 20 DEC 2019   Ensemble Members: GFS 20
Start Time: 2019121300Z Tau: 168   Approved for public access. Distribution is unlimited.

UNCLASSIFIED

NOAA ensemble forecast using 20 members at 168 hours, showing the probability of the wind speed being greater than 20kts

WEATHER APPS & WEBSITES

There are many internet sites giving a specific location service, where you enter your exact location and you get a forecast for that particular point. These are usually fine, especially at sea, but it's important to remember that any exact location forecast will be an interpolation of the forecast data at the grid point co-ordinates, which may be up to 30 miles away. There is usually no account taken of local topography, which can make a significant difference especially in harbours and close inshore. Always try to make use of the best resolution data available – the difference in detail between a half degree (56km) and a 4km resolution is significant.

A large number of these sites use as a base the freely available model output data from a national agency, often using the Global Forecast System (GFS) model from NOAA (the USA's National Oceanic & Atmospheric Administration) which has a horizontal resolution of 28km, a quarter of a degree. This means that if you enter a coastal location, say Falmouth Bay in the SW of England (see opposite) the final interpolation that you get may have input from 4 very different winds.

In this example there may be a northwesterly sea breeze just making its way inshore for the NW point, almost calm inland in the NE point, light southwesterly coming up the Channel in the SE and SW points. These will all have some weight at the desired location – where the actual wind may well be a light southeasterly, veering south, sea breeze.

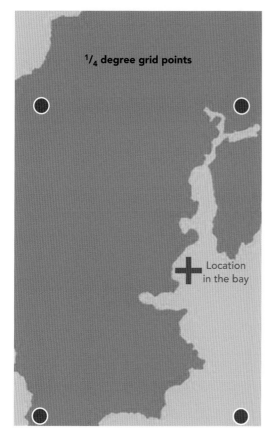 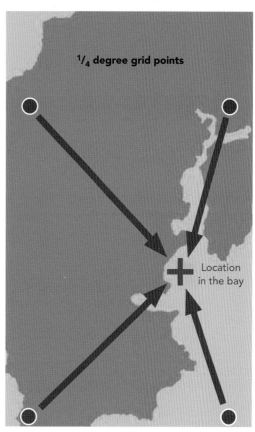

Quarter degree (28km) grid points around Falmouth, UK (left), and how their conditions are combined to give a forecast for a specified location in Falmouth Bay (right)

This interpolation is better with higher resolution, but even if you go down to the 1.5km resolution offered by the Met Office you still don't capture everything. The chart opposite shows how the wind funnelling up the east side of Carrick Roads in the UK is too small a feature to be picked up even at this level of resolution – it's a sub-grid feature.

Carrick Roads with a 1.5km grid on top: the way the southwesterly wind is funnelled and accelerated along the east side is not picked up by the model – it's a sub-grid feature

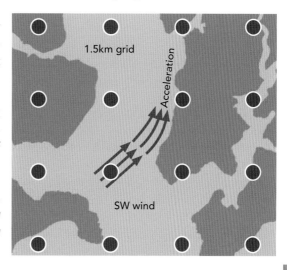

Another excellent example of this in practice is Sugar Loaf in Guanabara Bay, the sailing venue of the 2016 Olympics in Rio de Janeiro. This peak, 600m high and about 300m wide, was at what was usually the windward end of the Medal Race course area, and the single most significant topographic feature in the venue. This didn't show up at all on the models, even the 1km ones used. This is not a criticism of the technique, it's an excellent example of the fact that if a feature is small enough to fit into a grid square then it's effectively invisible as far as the model goes.

Sugar Loaf in Rio de Janeiro with an onshore breeze breaking over and around it

GMDSS WEATHER INFORMATION

The oceans are split into forecast areas (MetAreas) according to the World Meteorological Organisation (WMO) Marine Broadcast System for the Global Maritime Distress and Safety System.

The individual MetAreas are split into individual forecast areas, which in Met Area 1 are the UK Shipping Forecast areas. A text forecast is issued at least twice a day for each forecast area and can be used to build up a good picture of the weather systems and conditions in the area. The format is very much like the UK Met Office's Shipping Forecast. You do need a satellite receiver to get this, but the Inmarsat-C equipment is robust, small and generally very reliable. It doesn't use a directional dish and can only do text information.

THE BEAUFORT SCALE

This was devised by Francis Beaufort (later Rear Admiral Sir Francis Beaufort) in 1805 and was used to standardise wind observations throughout the Royal Navy at the time. The wind speed bands are devised to relate to the effects of the wind on the sails of a frigate.

Force 0	0-1kts	Calm	Sea like a mirror. Smoke rises vertically.
Force 1	1-3kts	Light air	Ripples have appearance of scales on water. Smoke drift and flags indicate direction.
Force 2	4-6kts	Light breeze	Small wavelets with glassy crests. Wind can be felt on the face. Flags indicate direction.
Force 3	7-10kts	Gentle breeze	Large wavelets with crests beginning to break producing scattered white horses.
Force 4	11-16kts	Moderate breeze	Small waves, becoming larger; frequent white horses. Keelboats require more work to keep balanced.
Force 5	17-21kts	Fresh winds	Moderate waves with regular white horses formed with spray. Flags fly horizontally.
Force 6	22-27kts	Strong winds	Large waves with white foam crests and spray are extensive.
Force 7	28-33kts	Near gale	Sea heaps up and white foam from breaking waves begins to be blown in streaks with the wind.
Force 8	34-40kts	Gale	Moderately high waves of greater length; edges of crests begin to break into spindrift. The foam is blown in well-marked streaks along the direction of the wind.
Force 9	41-47kts	Severe gale	High waves. Dense streaks of foam along the direction of the wind. Crests of waves begin to topple, tumble and roll over. Spray may affect visibility.
Force 10	48-55kts	Storm	Very high waves with long over-hanging crests. The resulting foam is blown in dense white streaks along the direction of the wind. The surface of the sea takes on a white appearance. The 'tumbling' of the sea becomes heavy and shock-like. Visibility affected.
Force 11	56-63kts	Violent storm	Exceptionally high waves (small and medium-size ships might be for a time lost to view behind the waves). The sea is completely covered with long white patches of foam lying along the direction of the wind. Everywhere the edges of the wave crests are blown into froth. Visibility affected.
Force 12	64-71kts	Hurricane	The air is filled with foam and spray. Sea completely white with driving spray; visibility very seriously affected.

SHIPPING FORECASTS – GENERAL TERMS

TIMING

The terms *imminent*, *soon* and *later* refer to the TIME OF ISSUE, not when you heard it!

	6hrs	12hrs	

Time of issue: the reference time of the forecast

Imminent: within 6 hours

Soon: 6-12 hours

Later: after 12 hours

WIND WARNINGS

Strong wind warnings: Average wind Beaufort F6 or F7 in that sea area
Gale warnings: Average wind Beaufort F8 or above in that sea area

SYSTEM SPEED

System speed in the General Synopsis – how fast the lows are travelling

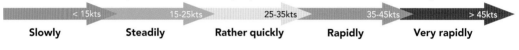

< 15kts	15-25kts	25-35kts	35-45kts	> 45kts
Slowly	**Steadily**	**Rather quickly**	**Rapidly**	**Very rapidly**

HIGHS & LOWS

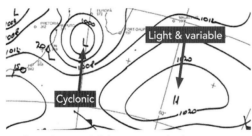

Light & Variable: very little pressure gradient, e.g. the centre of a high
Cyclonic: usually the centre of a low

WIND DIRECTION CHANGES

Veering: changing direction clockwise (W veering N here)

Backing: changing direction anti-clockwise (N backing W here)

VISIBILITY

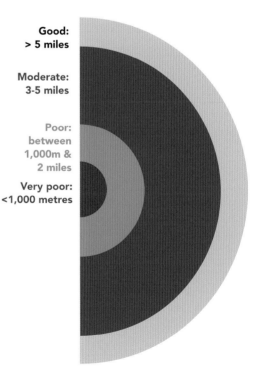

Good: > 5 miles

Moderate: 3-5 miles

Poor: between 1,000m & 2 miles

Very poor: <1,000 metres

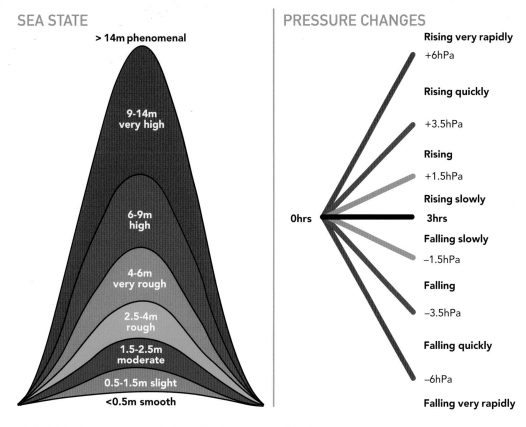

SEA STATE

> 14m phenomenal

9-14m
very high

6-9m
high

4-6m
very rough

2.5-4m
rough

1.5-2.5m
moderate

0.5-1.5m slight

<0.5m smooth

PRESSURE CHANGES

Rising very rapidly

+6hPa

Rising quickly

+3.5hPa

Rising

+1.5hPa

Rising slowly

Ohrs ———— 3hrs

Falling slowly

−1.5hPa

Falling

−3.5hPa

Falling quickly

−6hPa

Falling very rapidly

TAKING DOWN THE SHIPPING FORECAST

The BBC's Shipping Forecast is excellent for the North Sea, around the UK and down across Biscay to Spain and Portugal. Around the world local coastguard agencies often do something similar, so check with the national weather service website wherever you are.

Taking the shipping forecast down is a matter of practice and of developing your own shorthand. There are of course official abbreviations for all of these – however, my own shorthand produces the following:

"*Viking: south west 5 veering north west 5 increasing 7 later, squally showers, moderate occasionally poor*" becomes:

V: SW5 v NW5↑7 l sq sh m (p)

"*Dogger: north 4 or 5, occasionally 6 or 7 in east, fair, good*" becomes:

Dog N4/5 (6/7 in E) f g

I use somewhat dubious single letter abbreviations, up and down arrows, and whenever the forecaster says 'occasionally', brackets. Feel free to make your own system up – the key is a bit of practice. If it all goes horribly wrong just call the coastguard – they would far rather you have a forecast than not.

Try to get the sea areas around your area too, especially the ones to the west in the UK, as the weather systems usually travel from west to east.

3
MID-LATITUDE DEPRESSIONS

THE GENERAL PATH OF LOWS

The Jet Stream is a good indicator of the track of these low pressure systems, sometimes called the 'storm track', and this is why most of the weather at about 45° to 55° north or south of the Equator is brought by these mid-latitude systems.

The Jet Stream flows along the zone of greatest temperature difference in the atmosphere, where the relatively warm and wet air from the Tropics meets the relatively cold and dry air from the Poles – often known as the Polar Front.

The Jet Stream at 500hPa, about halfway up the troposphere, is shown opposite for the Northern and Southern Hemispheres for early January 2011. It can be seen that in the Northern Hemisphere it is much closer to the Equator – it is midwinter here, and Europe is in the grip of some very cold weather as depressions came in off the Atlantic to mix with cold Arctic air from the north. In the Southern Hemisphere, the Jet Stream is further away from the Equator as it is summer here with the depressions much further south, closer to the Pole, than in winter.

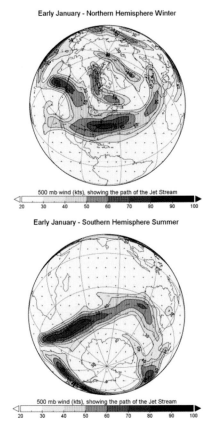

The Jet Streams shown by wind speed (kts) at 500hPa in early January 2011 for the Northern (top) and Southern (bottom) Hemispheres

HOW LOWS FORM

If the Jet Stream gives us an idea of where the depressions will track, the next thing to do is to look at how they are formed.

They tend to form where there is a large temperature difference over a relatively short distance, and the Polar Front is just that area. Also, the low pressure at the centre of a surface low means that the incoming air circulating around it at the surface converges towards the centre. This converging air has to go somewhere, and that is up. If air is coming in at the bottom it has to go out at the top, so an area of rising air with some upper level divergence below the top of the troposphere is important to allow this surface convergence to continue. Without air spreading out of the top of the low, air is blocked from converging in at the bottom.

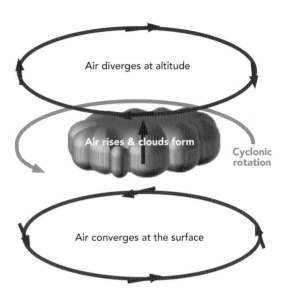

Surface convergence and upper level divergence in the Northern Hemisphere

THE UPPER LEVEL CHARTS TO SEE RISING & FALLING AIR

Once above the surface, where the atmosphere is described in terms of lines of equal pressure – isobars – the description changes from one of pressure at a certain height to that of the height of a particular pressure. This is why charts of the 500mbar height are given in metres. This allows us to see troughs and ridges in the upper

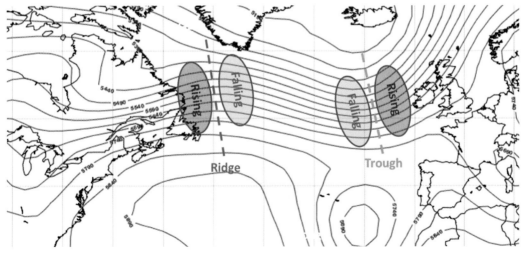

A 500hPa geopotential height chart showing a ridge, a trough and the rising and falling air ahead and behind them

atmosphere and, as the previous diagram shows, air rises going up to a ridge and falls after it, and it falls approaching a trough and rises after it – just like you would walking through valleys and over ridges on the ground using a contour map.

This means that upstream of a ridge and downstream of a trough there will be rising air which will aid surface convergence and the formation of clouds and potentially rain – this is why upper level troughs are usually shown on surface pressure charts, as there will probably be cloudy and rainy weather under them. This shows that if we have an area of surface convergence either upstream of a ridge or downstream of a trough, the upper atmosphere will help to keep this going and even increase it.

THE JET STREAM'S EFFECT ON CONVERGENCE & DIVERGENCE

Upper level air accelerates into the Jet Entrance and decelerates out of the Jet Exit, as shown below.

The Jet Stream at 200 hPa, December 21st 2019

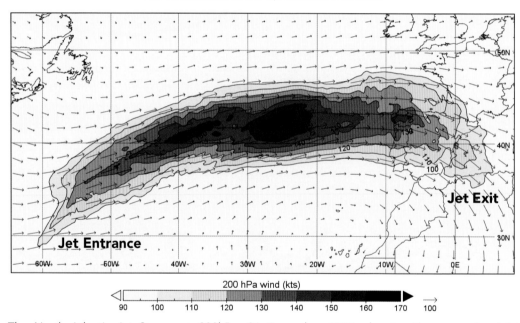

The North Atlantic Jet Stream at 200hPa, 21 December 2019, showing the upper level jet accelerating into the fastest part of it then decelerating as it exits the jet

In general, air parcels will travel along the lines of equal geopotential height when there is no acceleration or deceleration (this simplification ignores any friction effects, which decrease from the surface). In this simplified universe, the individual air parcels have two effects acting on them here – the pressure gradient force pulling them towards the Pole, and the Coriolis Effect pushing them away from it (p15).

The diagram opposite shows that coming into the Jet Entrance the height contours get closer together, giving a larger pressure gradient. Looking at the parcel on the central contour, the stages are:

1. The pressure gradient (red arrow) matched the Coriolis Effect (purple arrow) and the parcel moves east.
2. The pressure gradient increases as the contours get closer, so the parcel is pulled north. The Coriolis Effect moves forward as it's always at 90° to the motion, so the parcel accelerates.
3. The Coriolis Effect increases with speed to balance the pressure, and a faster equilibrium is reached.

This causes convergence in the left-hand side of the Jet Entrance, and divergence in the right-hand side (with reference to the direction of flow).

At the Jet Exit the opposite occurs:

4. The pressure gradient and the Coriolis Effect are balanced, with the parcel moving east.
5. The pressure gradient decreases so the parcel moves south. The Coriolis Effect moves backwards with this as it's always at 90° to the motion, so the parcel decelerates.
6. The Coriolis Effect decreases with speed to balance the pressure, reaching a slower equilibrium.

This causes convergence in the right-hand side of the Jet Exit, and divergence in the left-hand side (with reference to the direction of flow).

So, if there is surface convergence beneath a right Jet Entrance or a left Jet Exit region then the upper level dynamics will help that convergence to continue and even increase.

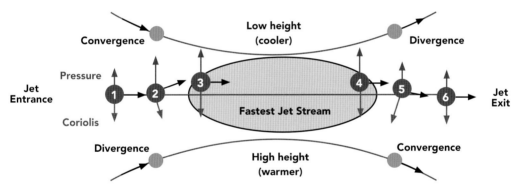

Schematic of how an air parcel is affected by Jet Entrance and Exit zones, causing upper level convergence and divergence

The same thing happens as a mirror image in the Southern Hemisphere, with the Jet Entrance convergence to the south & the Jet Exit convergence to the north.

LOWS DEVELOPING & FILLING IN 3 DIMENSIONS

The 8 October (left column overleaf) begins with a new low forming over Newfoundland (A) and a mature low just east of Iceland (B). Low A is upstream of a ridge and its surface convergence should therefore be helped by the rising air at the 500hPa level. It is forming up just east of the left-hand Jet Entrance, so this is either neutral or slightly hindering development. With 2 out of 3 levels helping, this low should deepen and develop.

On the other side of the Atlantic low B is in the left Jet Entrance region, and this should give convergence at the upper level, slowly shutting off the upward flow through the system. Also, there's hardly anything happening at the 500hPa level – this low should fill.

Looking at the situation 24 hours later (right column), it can be seen that this has happened – low A has deepened and, as it is now downstream of a trough with rising air above it, this should continue to deepen. Low B has filled and will continue to do so with some convergence above it from the left Jet Entrance region.

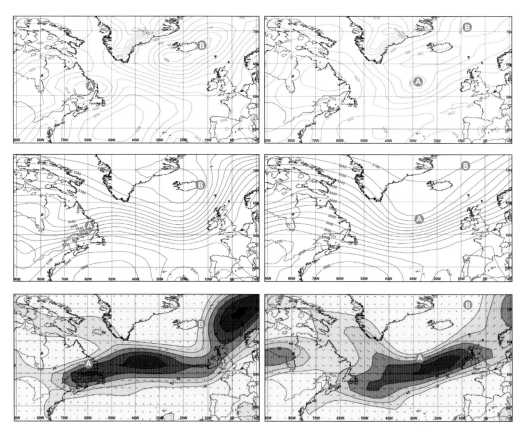

The surface isobars (top), 500hPa heights (middle) and Jet Stream winds (bottom) for the 8 (left) & 9 (right) October 2005

A QUICK SUMMARY SO FAR

A low pressure system is a three dimensional being, and needs convergence at the surface and divergence aloft to develop. The convergence at the surface often occurs in regions where warm, wet air meets cold dry air, and two examples of this are along the eastern seaboard of North America and on the western shores of the North Pacific from Taiwan to north of Japan.

Up aloft rising air happens downstream of an upper level trough ('climbing out' of the valley) and upstream of an upper level ridge ('climbing up' to the crest of the ridge). Also, upper level divergence occurs to the right of a Jet Entrance, and to the left of a Jet Exit in the Northern Hemisphere. If surface convergence occurs underneath rising air or upper level divergence, then the low has a good chance of 'spinning up' and deepening.

We haven't mentioned weather fronts yet – they come next.

DIFFERENT AIR MASSES

The air masses at work in the mid-latitudes (see below) are characterised by relative temperature, and relative dryness and wetness, and these are entirely dependent on where the air masses have been. The Northern Hemisphere is more affected by air masses moving over land than the Southern, purely because the Southern Hemisphere is mostly oceanic.

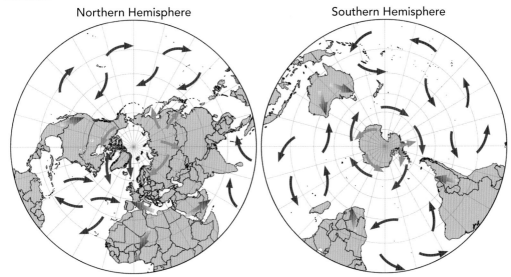

The different mid-latitude air masses and their origins

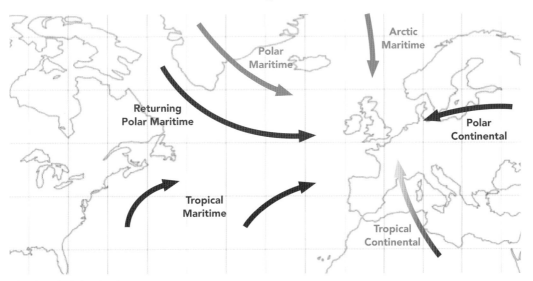

The North Atlantic air masses

- **Tropical Maritime Air:** Relatively warm and wet, with a long fetch over the Atlantic.
- **Tropical Continental Air:** Warm, but relatively dry.
- **Polar Continental Air:** Cold (very cold in winter) and dry – in the UK & Europe, think of those cold crisp winter days with easterly winds blowing in. (This type of air doesn't occur in the Southern Hemisphere as there are no large mid-latitude continental areas for it to blow over.)

- **Arctic / Antarctic Maritime Air:** Also cold, but with slightly more moisture as it has travelled over some sea.
- **Polar Maritime Air:** Cold, with yet more moisture due to the longer fetch over the relatively warmer ocean (think of the Gulf Stream fanning out over the North Atlantic).
- **Returning Polar Maritime Air:** This is Maritime Polar Air that's come more towards the Equator, generally over a warmer patch of water (e.g. the Gulf Stream).

FRONTAL SYSTEMS

A frontal system is a low pressure system that develops with two different air masses, and the fronts are merely the leading edges of these air masses as they rotate around the low. Looking at a typical low forming in the western Atlantic, the warm and wet Tropical Maritime air mass moves in from the southwest, while the cold and dry Polar Maritime or Returning Polar Maritime Air comes down from the Arctic, effectively bringing conveyor belts of different types of air moving on either side of the Polar Front.

This Polar Front is, broadly speaking, under the Jet Stream, and is the place where most mid-latitude frontal depressions start. The chart opposite shows the Polar Front extending all the way across the Atlantic from south of Newfoundland to the Baltic. Along the Polar Front it changes from a warm front to a cold front and back again on several occasions – this indicates the general direction of the air mass movement. Where it's a cold front the colder, drier air is moving forward, where it's a warm front the warmer wetter air is moving forward.

The Southern Hemisphere has a similar Polar Front, generally seen linking depressions together, as shown in the chart opposite.

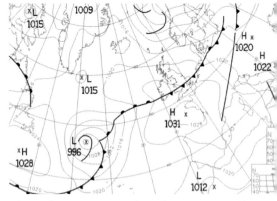

The Polar Front extending from 36°N 050°W to 55°N 020°E (Met Office, contains public sector information licensed under the Open Government Licence v1.0.)

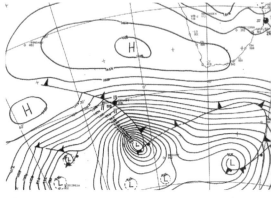

The Polar Front extending along 35-48°S linking the lows (South African Weather Service)

The first stage in the development of a low occurs when the relatively warm and wet Tropical Maritime Air starts to push polewards slightly, with the cold and dry Polar Air pushing slightly equatorwards. This creates a wave in the Polar Front (see below) and the start of the warm and cold fronts at the front edge of their respective air masses.

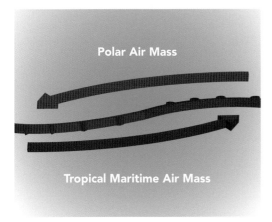

Polar Air Mass

Tropical Maritime Air Mass

A wave starting in the Northern Hemisphere Polar Front

Once the low becomes more mature and wind starts to rotate around the centre then the air coming from the different air masses forms various streams, or conveyor belts of different air (see below). The warm air coming from the Tropics rises above the colder, drier air ahead of it – and this gives rise to the **warm front**. The dry conveyor belt brings colder, drier Polar Air and this butts up against the warm tropical air to form the **cold front**. The area in between them is the **warm sector**. These fronts are where the majority of our 'weather' comes from – rain, hail, snow, changing winds and all the other vagaries of Mother Nature. We will look at these in more detail later.

As the low develops further and then starts to fill, the dry conveyor belt of air behind the cold front meets up with the cold conveyor belt ahead of the warm front to form an occluded front – this basically lifts any remaining warm sector air above it and draws the cold and warm fronts together like a closing zip fastener.

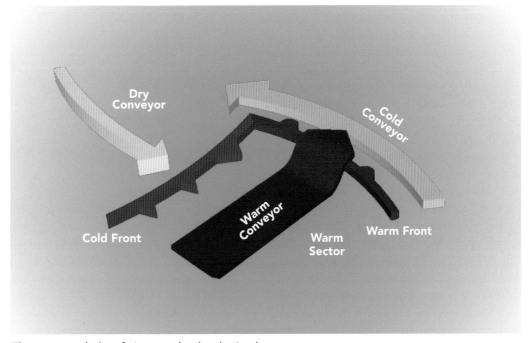

Dry Conveyor

Cold Conveyor

Warm Conveyor

Cold Front

Warm Sector

Warm Front

The conveyor belts of air around a developing low

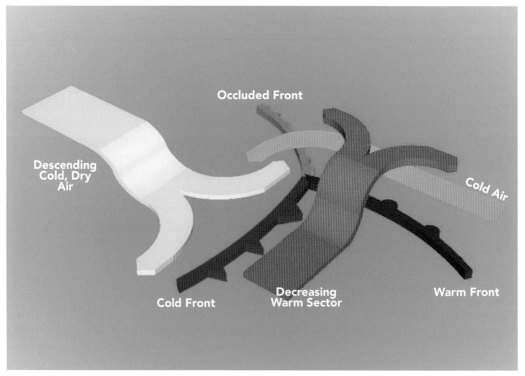

The cold front catching up with the warm front to form an occluded front

This also explains why the cold front catches up the warm front. The warm sector air is pushed up the slope of the warm front, and as it does so the air cools, causing water to condense out and form the sequence of warm front clouds. By the time the warm sector air makes it to the top of the slope of the front, it has lost almost all of its moisture and is cold – so has become like the relatively cold & dry air ahead of the warm front. This means that the warm sector air is effectively pushed up and out of the warm sector – eventually the cold front will catch up.

Let's look at an example in the North Atlantic where this often happens just off the eastern seaboard of the North American land mass, where there's a large temperature contrast between the Tropical Maritime air from the south & the Arctic Maritime air from the north (but this is not limited to this area).

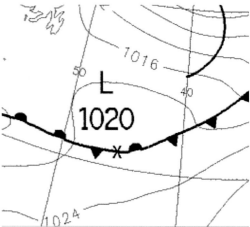

1. A wave starts southeast of Newfoundland, marked by the forecaster as a low with a central pressure of 1,020hPa. This illustrates how lows are not defined by their central pressures being less than a certain level, it's all about how the air flows around and into them. In this case the change in the front (cold front to the west, warm front to the east) shows cyclonic flow just around the central X.

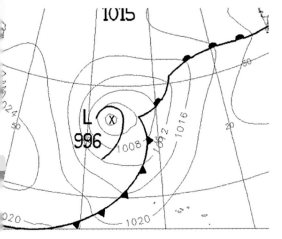

2. Three days later the wave in the Polar Front has developed into a closed circulation with a definite warm front, cold front and a warm sector between the two. By closed circulation we mean the forming of closed isobars going into the centre of the low, with a complete 360° circulation of airflow around the centre of the low at surface.

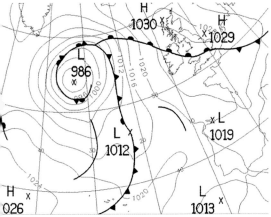

3. The system is developing into a classic North Atlantic low, with an occluded front being wrapped around the centre of the low by the cold air conveyor from the east and the descending cold dry air from the west and the south. Also, note the wave just starting along the trailing cold front marked as 1,012hPa – this could spin up into a low in its own right, called a secondary depression. (Met Office, contains public sector information licensed under the Open Government Licence v1.0.)

WINDS AROUND THE LOW

As air circulates around a low pressure centre it is affected (simplistically) by two forces – the pressure gradient force taking it in towards the centre, and the Coriolis Effect trying to push it to the right (in the Northern Hemisphere) and the left (in the Southern Hemisphere). At the surface the wind is affected by surface friction, which slows the air parcels down. This reduction in speed reduces the Coriolis force on them and hence they converge towards the centre of the low – this is why lows in the Southern Hemisphere rotate clockwise, and in the Northern Hemisphere anti-clockwise.

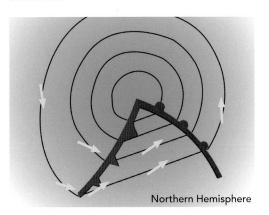

Northern Hemisphere

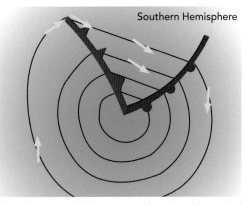

Southern Hemisphere

A surface analysis chart showing the wind direction going in towards the centre of a Northern (top) & Southern (bottom) Hemisphere low

41

Friction also depends on the type of surface, and it makes sense that water gives less friction than land. At surface level, therefore, the wind angles in by about 15° towards the centre of the low, compared to about 30° over land. So, to work out which way the wind's blowing, merely look at the direction of the isobars, and angle the wind in by about 15° if you're at sea, and by about 30° if you're on land.

The wind strength depends on the pressure gradient – the closer the isobars are together, the stronger it will be. The pressure tendency is very important here – *if the pressure falls or rises more than 1hPa per hour (or 3hPa in 3 hours) then strong winds are to be expected.*

SURFACE CONDITIONS AS THE LOW PASSES OVER

The conditions at the surface depend on the air mass in which the observer is, and any fronts that may be passing overhead. Let's look at a cross section through a typical low (see below). The cross section is taken along the direction of travel of the system, and so can be used as a guide to the general flow of conditions as they pass overhead.

Looking at the overall shape, the warm sector is deeper than the colder air masses ahead and behind it, which makes sense as it is warmer and therefore will expand more. The tropopause is the top

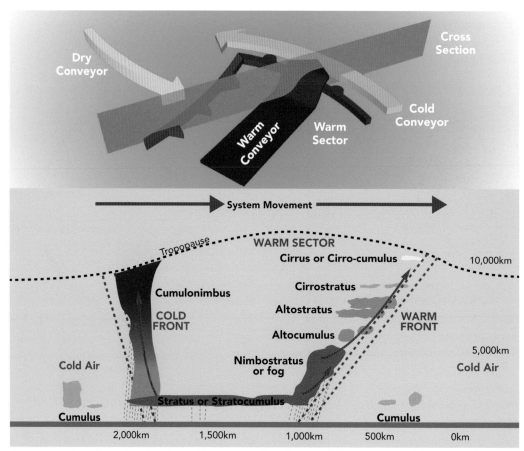

A cross section through a Northern Hemisphere low (top) and the vertical activity along that cross section (bottom)

of the troposphere and is the dividing line between the troposphere and the stratosphere. Also, note that the horizontal and vertical scales are quite different, and the slope of both the cold and warm fronts is exaggerated.

THE WARM FRONT

This is the leading edge of the warm conveyor, and the front of the warm sector. As such the warm air will climb up over the cold conveyor ahead of it and, as it rises, it will cool and the moisture in it will condense to form clouds and then rain. The thickness of the clouds decreases with altitude, starting with nimbostratus (or fog – which is just cloud at ground level), then altocumulus, altostratus, cirrostratus and cirrus clouds. So, if you are ahead of one of these, the visibility will be quite good initially, as you will be in relatively cold, dry air, and there will be some light stratus or cumulus cloud around.

Several hundred kilometres before the surface front reaches you, high level wispy cirrus clouds will appear, getting lower and thicker until the actual front arrives at surface together with rain and possibly fog. The wind will be from the south or even southeast in the Northern Hemisphere, and generally from the north to northeast in the Southern, and the barometer will be steadily falling. The air temperature will be cooler ahead of the warm front but, before it clouds over, the Sun will make for more pleasant conditions.

At the warm front the wind will veer towards the southwest in the Northern Hemisphere and back towards the northwest in the Southern, the rain will be at its heaviest to date before easing off to a drizzle or less, visibility will be poor in fog or rain, and the barometer will stop falling so quickly.

THE WARM SECTOR

This is part of a single air mass, so the conditions will be steadier here. The warm sector is where the warm conveyor is, so the air will be relatively warm and wet. There may well be low stratus cloud or some fog with occasional rain or drizzle, and this will make the temperature feel cool as the Sun is blocked, even if the air temperature is up. This level of moisture in the air will give moderate visibility, which may be poor if it rains.

The wind will be steady from around the southwest in the Northern Hemisphere, northwest in the Southern, and the barometer will also be steady, generally either rising or falling very slowly. If it's falling, it may well be that the entire low is deepening. This sector is usually good for sailing, but not for sunbathing.

THE COLD FRONT

The cold front is a very different animal to the warm front. As the air mass is cold and dry, it cannot climb up and over the warm sector air mass, so all the interaction between the two air masses happens in a more vertical plane, potentially allowing the formation of massive cumulonimbus clouds fed by warm updrafts from the warm sector forced up by cold air trying to push in underneath. Just ahead of the front there may be a sudden dip in pressure by 1 or 2hPa, but this often goes unnoticed as there are more important things to do than look at the barometer – putting reefs in, for example. Conditions just ahead of and under the front can be severe, with strong, cold gusts coming off the edges of the cumulonimbus clouds, and heavy rain or hail and electrical storms all possible. As a result of all this, visibility may be very poor under the front itself.

After the cold front has passed, however, the wind will veer again towards the west or northwest in the Northern Hemisphere and back towards the southwest in the Southern, the skies will clear almost immediately, and as the air is now part of the cold, dry air mass the visibility will be excellent and there may be some scenic cumulus clouds if any. The wind may not yet decrease in strength, however – that depends on the isobar spacing. The pressure will now start to increase however, so calmer weather will be on the way.

THE END OF A DEPRESSION – OCCLUSIONS

As the whole system becomes more mature the cold front will start to catch up with the warm front, very much like a zipper being done up (see p39). This forms an occluded front and results in what's left of the warm sector being pushed up above the preceding and following cold air masses which now join up (see below). The example shown is a warm occlusion because the air advancing faster behind the cold front is warmer than the air ahead of the warm front. If it was the other way around, with the air behind the cold front colder than the air ahead of the warm

front, it would be a cold occlusion. From the observer's point of view beneath them, they're both wet.

As all this warm wet air is lifted, it cools, causing water vapour to condense as the air cools to appear in the form of a persistent miserable drizzle and low level cloud. As this is towards the end of the frontal system's life it's normally not very energetic, just wet.

SECONDARY DEPRESSIONS

Occasionally one of these will develop quickly on the trailing edge of the cold front of a mature depression, and they can be both strong and fast moving (the obvious example is the Fastnet Race storm of 1979).

An example is the best way to illustrate this, with the charts opposite showing a complex occluding low (Low A) trailing a cold front down to a secondary low (Low B), which quickly develops into a strong system in its own right over 24 hours, still with its own long trailing cold front as a continuation of the Polar Front reaching across the Atlantic.

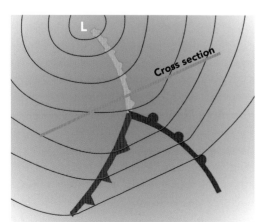
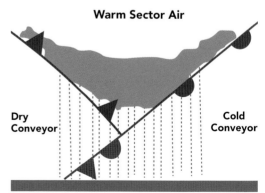

Occluding low on a synoptic chart (left) with a vertical cross-section (right) marked in green on the synoptic chart; the dry conveyor air behind the cold front is warmer in this case so it rises above the colder air ahead of the warm front – in this case a warm occlusion

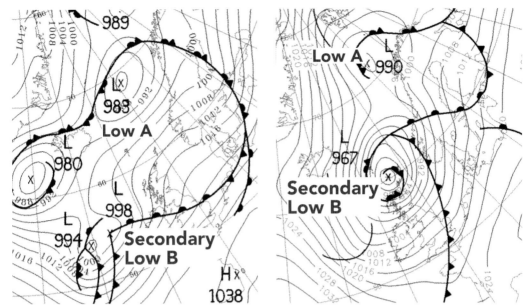

A secondary depression (Low B) developing on the trailing cold front of an occluding depression (Low A); the right panel is 24 hours after the left (Met Office, contains public sector information licensed under the Open Government Licence v1.0.)

HEAT LOWS

A heat low usually develops over an area of land that is significantly hotter than the seas around it, and a Northern Hemisphere example of this is the low often sitting over the Iberian Peninsula. The pressure in the centre of these will not be that low, but they are characterised by strong convection and this shows up on the thermal infra-red images as very white (and therefore cold and high) clouds.

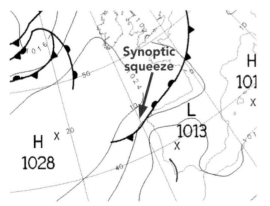

Synoptic chart of a heat low over the Iberian Peninsula (left: Met Office) and the corresponding thermal infra-red image (right: image courtersy of Unviersity of Dundee Archive Services); there's a deep area of white, and therefore cold and high clouds, corresponding to the X marking the centre of rotation on the synoptic chart; the isobars are squeezed between the high and the low around Cape Finisterre

When they start up they are in the same air mass and so do not have fronts, so rather than bands of rain they tend to have deep convective clouds with much more squally weather. A significant effect on the wind occurs as they push up against any nearby ocean high: causing an increase in the pressure gradient and therefore the wind over what can be a small geographic area. This is typically what happens down the Portuguese coast, and it is common in summer to have light winds across Biscay, then 20 knots or more from the north as you get to Finisterre and go further south.

In the Southern Hemisphere these also develop over hotter coastal areas, such as the lows that develop inland in Brazil in the Parana region south of Rio de Janeiro which are known as Sudestada. These often move out to sea along cold fronts – more on this later.

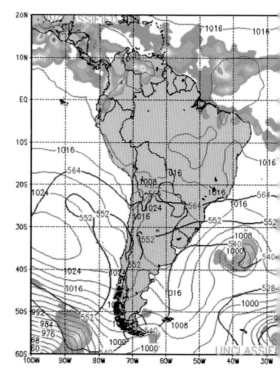

Sea level pressure (hPa) and rainfall (mm/6 hours) for South America (above) and the matching thermal infra-red image (left: image courtesy of University of Dundee Archive Services) showing a Sudestada at 39°S 038°W; this has travelled out to sea on the cold front leading down to the Southern Ocean low off to the southeast

PRECIPITATION – WILL IT BE RAIN, SNOW OR SLEET?

Rain often starts out as snow, and melts on the way down as the air temperature increases. From this we can say that if it reaches the ground as snow then the atmosphere must be cold enough to prevent it from melting. A good indicator of this is the thickness of the layer from 1,000hPa to 500hPa, which is roughly the thickness of the lower half of the atmosphere by mass. This is usually measured in decametres and the smaller this thickness is, the denser and therefore the colder the atmosphere is. As a general rule of thumb, if the 1,000hPa to 500hPa thickness is:

- Less than 528dm: then any precipitation will be as snow
- Between 528 and 546dm: it will be a rather unpleasant mixture of sleet, snow and rain
- More than 546dm: it will be rain

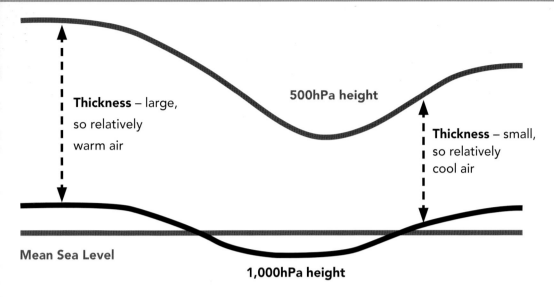

Thickness – large, so relatively warm air

500hPa height

Thickness – small, so relatively cool air

Mean Sea Level

1,000hPa height

The 1,000hPa height (black) is usually close to the surface (mean sea level here): where it dips below the surface it implies a mean sea level pressure less than 1,000hPa; the thickness is the difference in height between the 1,000hPa and 500hPa (red) heights: this is bigger when the air is warmer, less when it's cooler

In the forecast chart (right) the 528dm line shows the tongue of cold Polar Air curling into the low, while the red 546dm line borders the relatively warmer air closer to the Equator. In this example, precipitation in northern Scotland will be snow, through most of England and across the central North Sea sleety rain, then along the south coast of England, Cornwall and Western Europe it'll be rain.

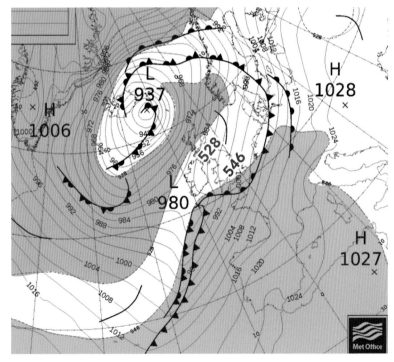

Forecast chart with the 528dm thickness line showing the edge of the blue 'snow' zone, the 546dm line the edge of the red 'rain' zone (Met Office, contains public sector information licensed under the Open Government Licence v1.0.)

HAIL

Hail occurs all over the world, whatever temperature the air at surface is. Hail is made up of rain drops that have been kept up above the freezing height by strong updrafts.

Strong updrafts are generated in deep squall clouds and tropical depressions in the Tropics, and in tall cumulonimbus clouds along cold fronts in the extra-tropical regions. Because the cloud is tall, a significant proportion of it will be above the freezing level, and any tiny droplets will actually be ice crystals or supercooled droplets. These will be bounced around in the strong updrafts and will accrete more and more ice, becoming larger and therefore heavier.

After a while the weight of the larger ice crystal (proportional to the cube of its radius) will become stronger than the upwards force provided by the updrafts (depends on its surface area, so proportional to the square of the radius) and it will fall as a hailstone. If it is large enough then not all of it will melt by the time it gets to the surface, and the un-melted bit is what we see as a hailstone.

Deep, dark cumulonimbus cloud – perfect for hail development

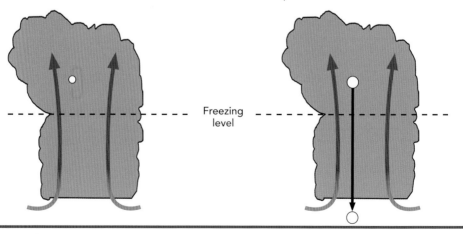

Freezing level

A small ice crystal bounces around in a tall cumulus cloud (left), held up there by the strong updrafts; after a while it gets big enough so that its weight is more than the upward force of the air moving up around it, and it falls to the surface as a hailstone (right)

4

HIGHS, LOWS & THE JET STREAM – HOW THEY INTERACT

HIGH PRESSURE SYSTEMS

As we have seen, high pressure systems occur where there is upper level convergence and lower level divergence. This means that air is coming into a high at the upper levels, descending, and then rotating out at the surface (clockwise in the Northern Hemisphere, anticlockwise in the Southern Hemisphere).

They are more stable than low pressure systems and can stay in the same general area for days or more. Because the high has descending air in it, this air will usually have started off high up in the troposphere where pressure, and therefore temperature and the amount of water vapour are low. As it descends the pressure will increase and with it the temperature, but as there is no source of moisture the relative humidity will keep decreasing, so the air will become relatively dry as it descends (see p19) – this means that it will be clear with good visibility.

The surface beneath it will become heated by the Sun as there are no upper level clouds in the way, and this causes the lowest part of the troposphere to rise – we have convection. This rising air meets and is capped by the descending air from above, which leads to what is known as an inversion where the convection due to the Sun's heating is trapped below a column of descending air. This explains why high pressure days in summer, especially along the coast and at sea, are often characterised by low level stratus clouds and hazy conditions at surface.

During the winter, the surface heating is much less than in the summer, so the days are characterised by beautifully clear skies and often bitingly low temperatures at night as there is no cloud cover to keep what little heat there is in.

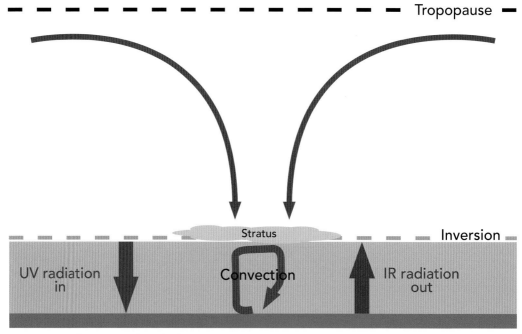

An inversion forming under a high pressure system

THE JET STREAM & THE PATH OF LOWS

Weather forecasts tend to lose detail after about 5 days, but mostly the general trend of large features away from the direct influence of the surface, like the Jet Stream, are well forecast. This is particularly useful in the mid-latitudes, as this generally shows us the path of the lows. A useful parameter is just one contour of the 500hPa height (the 5,640m) which generally runs equatorward of the low centres.

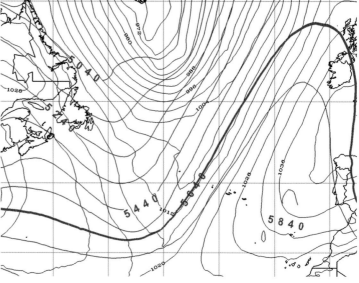

500hPa height (m, red) and mean sea level pressure isobars (hPa, black): the 5,640m height contour is emphasised as a proxy for the centre of the Jet Stream: lows are on the poleward side of the 5,640m contour, highs on the equatorward side

What this means is that the lows will tend to run just north of it in the Northern Hemisphere, and just south of it in the Southern. On the equatorward side of it we tend to get the high pressure systems (an exception to this being tropical lows – they develop on the equatorward side and often then recurve and transition to the higher latitudes).

This is very useful for medium range passage planning (sometimes up to 10 days ahead). Weather forecasts tend to get the general flow of systems correct, but the detail of when fronts are going to go over will change in time.

If you know that the Jet Stream will be bringing lows over for that period then you know that the general trend of wind will be from the west and there's likely to be some frontal activity.

THE BASIC INTERACTION OF HIGHS & LOWS

Lows are inherently unstable systems, with air converging at low level, rising and then diverging up high. Highs are far more stable, with air converging at altitude and then descending before diverging at the surface. Highs are also far slower moving than lows and tend to stay in the same place.

Looking at this example over the North Atlantic and Europe we can see that there are several lows and highs all jostling for position:

- The highs are relatively slow moving, so the western low will push up against the high over the UK to create strong southerly winds in between the two (red area labelled 1), which will get stronger as the low moves eastwards.
- The two lows over Europe will move further east, so the strong northeasterly winds over southern France and the Alps (red area labelled 2) will decrease as the isobars spread out.
- The two European lows will have an area of light or no wind in between them (blue area labelled 3), as will the ridge between the two highs (blue area labelled 4).
- Also, there is another 'flat spot' just north east of the Caribbean where there will be little or no wind (blue area labelled 5).

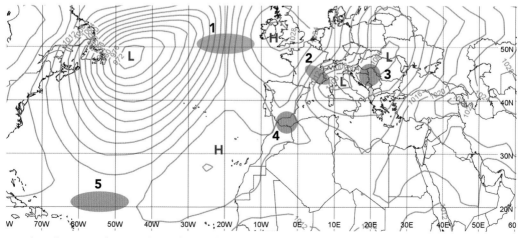

North Atlantic surface analysis (hPa), showing highs, lows and the areas of stronger wind (red shading) and lighter wind (blue shading) between the systems

As can be seen, the surface isobars give us a visual idea of the surface pressure gradient, and the steeper that gradient is, the stronger will be the wind. Conversely, any flat spots give little or no wind, even though they may be geographically close to areas of strong wind.

SYSTEM MOVEMENT IN THE NORTHERN HEMISPHERE

There's a lot more land north of the Equator, which extends a long way further polewards than it does south of it. This has a significant effect on the movement of the mid-ocean highs. These often get blocked on the eastern side of both Europe and of North America.

Taking a North Atlantic example (see opposite), we can see that with the Jet Stream going well north (looking at the **564dm contour** on the 500hPa height plot for Day 1) the surface high pushes right up over the UK towards Scandinavia. This is much the same for Day 3, and it's only until Day 7 that the Jet Stream moves south, cradling a new low across the Atlantic to finally bring westerlies up the Channel again. In fact, in this particular example, the blocking high had been in place for 10 days before this sequence started.

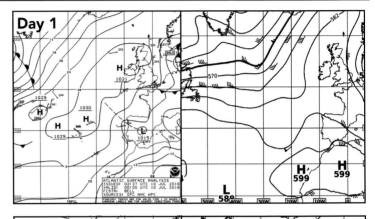

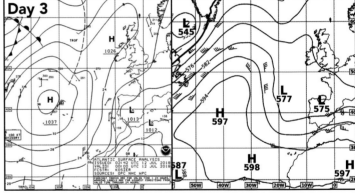

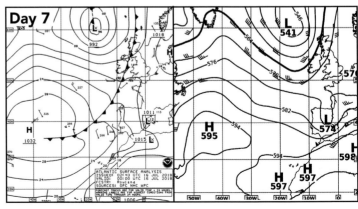

Surface analysis charts (left) and 500hPa charts (right, 564dm contour highlighted bold for middle of Jet Stream) for Days 1, 3 and 7 in the sequence

SYSTEM MOVEMENT IN THE SOUTHERN HEMISPHERE

The first basic of Southern Hemisphere weather is that lows and highs rotate the opposite direction to how they go in the Northern Hemisphere. This means that the lows rotate clockwise and the highs anticlockwise.

The other big difference is that the Southern Hemisphere has far less land than the Northern, and this allows the mid-ocean highs much more freedom of movement. Taking the example of the South Atlantic, the high generally moves slowly to the east. When it reaches Africa, rather than sitting there, not able to move because it's butting up against a continental land mass, it tends to slide south underneath the continent, as shown by this sequence of South African Weather Service analysis charts.

This sequence shows the high sliding round the bottom of Africa with a low then sweeping a cold front along behind it. These cold fronts give rise to 'southerly busters', where the wind can change direction by nearly 180° and build rapidly to 50kts or more over just a few minutes.

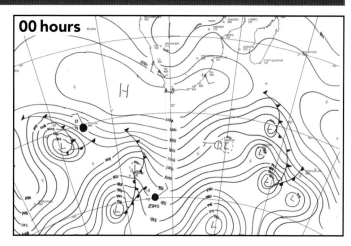

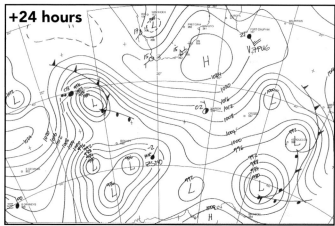

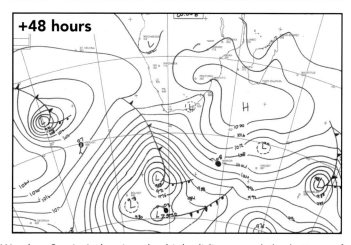

Synoptic charts (South African Weather Service) showing the high sliding round the bottom of Africa (top), leaving a gap along the Western Cape shore (middle) allowing a cold front to sweep along in between the first high and the next approaching system (bottom)

Around the bottom of Australia, a similar thing happens as well. Looking at the sequence below, the first thing to note is how the highs slide slowly east. Then, look how the cold front trailing towards the western end of the south coast (00-hours panel) meets up with a trough over Western Australia, with a low developing inland. 24 hours later this low is moving southeast down the front, and by 48 hours the front hammers through Bass Strait between Tasmania and the mainland, in this case bringing a reported 75kt southerly buster. By the 72-hour panel it's also moved east, and all is peaceful again.

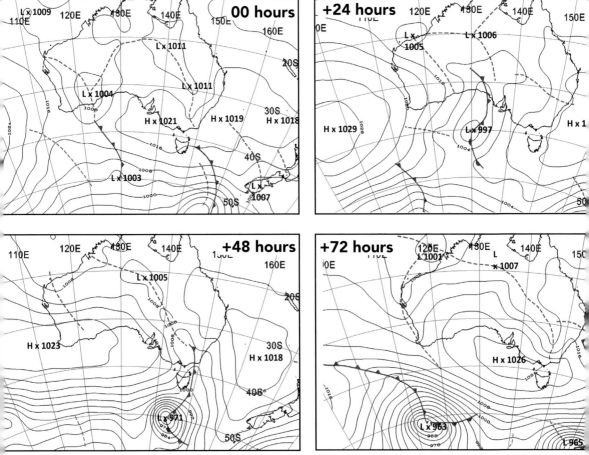

High sliding east into the Tasman Sea with a cold front trailing up towards the western side of the south coast (00 hours); the inland low moves out to sea down this front (+24 hours), and deepens (+48 hours) with a vigorous front going through Bass Strait; this brought a southerly buster with reported 75kt winds, and by +72 hours had cleared to the east

This process of lows starting on the coast or just inland and moving down trailing cold fronts happens up the South American coast (with the sudestada and pamperos, see p46), the South African coast and up the east coast of Australia as well. These lows can develop very quickly and bring rapidly changing conditions. The often large difference in moisture content and temperature of the Tropical Continental and Tropical Maritime air masses rotating into these lows only adds to their energy.

5
THE BOUNDARY LAYER

Moving up from the surface, the very lowest part of the atmosphere is called the boundary layer and this is the part which directly interacts with the Earth's surface. It's no more than 1,500-2,000m deep, often much less. The air in this layer is affected by friction with the surface, any pollution in the air will be concentrated here, and this is where we get local effects like sea breezes, land breezes and fog.

SEA BREEZE

This is the sailor's saviour on hot, still summer days when the country is sitting under an enormous high pressure system with very little overall pressure gradient and an early morning inversion layer above the cool dawn surface. It's caused by the way the land heats up faster than the sea:

- In the morning the land will heat up (a rise of about 3-4°C over sea surface temperature is sufficient to get it going) and by around lunch time the air above the land will have started to warm up and expand.
- As it does so it can only go one way – that's up and out to sea. It can't go inland because the air there is also expanding.
- This moving of air away from the land causes a localised low pressure onshore, and the air moving out to sea cools and

adds to the air there, forming a localised high pressure offshore – lo and behold, we now have a local thermal circulation going.

Dawn in Palma, March 2019: low inversion shown by dust and haze layer, with a light offshore wind taking scattered cloud out to sea

If there is a gentle offshore geostrophic wind above the boundary layer this helps matters along. This is a very localised version of the overall global circulation described on p11.

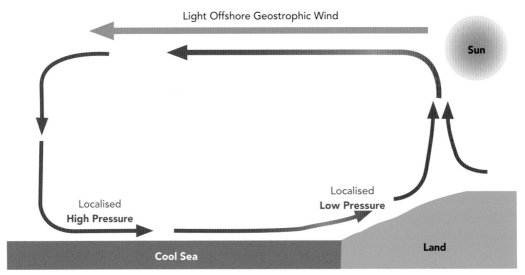

The onset of sea breeze with the morning Sun warming the land and thus the air above it; this expands out to sea causing a pressure difference, and this causes the onshore sea breeze

As the day moves on, the temperature difference between land and sea increases, driving the process more. Also, moist air coming back onto land will rise and as it does so the water vapour in it will condense to form a line of cumulus clouds along the coast.

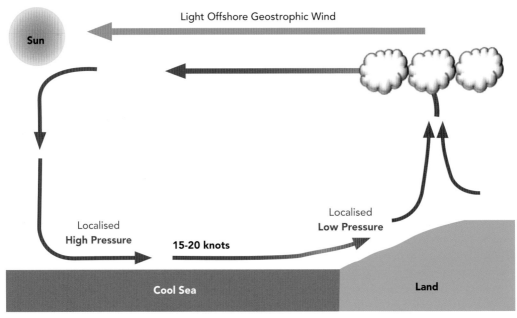

When the sea breeze is established there is usually a line of small cumulus along the coast which doesn't go out to sea

This effect can be felt several miles out to sea. It's generally not well forecast by the standard weather models (see p26) until the model resolution gets down to about 2km or less, so an understanding of what causes it and what you will see is very useful.

While the sea breeze generally starts off coming straight onshore it will be affected by Coriolis, and this means that in the Northern Hemisphere it veers right and in the Southern it backs left (assuming no other local effects are in play), generally by up to 30° over a 2-3 hour period in the warmest part of the afternoon from around 1300 to 1600 local time.

If the conditions are marginal and not obvious, for example, you have an offshore breeze but it's quite a cold day and you're not sure if the sea / land temperature difference is going to be enough, then look at the clouds.

These photos from Palma in March 2019 show this nicely:

- Small scraps of cumulus developing late morning as the land heats up and air starts to rise
- With a line of inland cumulus after noon as the sea breeze cell starts
- By mid-afternoon these clouds are thickest, indicating peak flow

Really important is that even though you'll see the inland cumulus tops move towards the sea (they are in the upper part of the cell), the clouds disappear rapidly as they get over the water and the air starts to subside.

Palma in March 2019: developing scraps of cumulus early on showing rising air (top), followed by a more organised line of inland cumulus as the cell develops (middle) and then thickest at its peak flow (bottom)

LAND BREEZE

Just as in the day the land heated up faster than the sea, so at night it will cool faster than the sea. This causes an opposite temperature imbalance, with the sea now warmer than the land, and so a circulation will develop the other way around.

As this is not driven by the Sun but by heat radiating from the cooling land it is a much weaker phenomenon than a sea breeze.

This flow is often chanelled down valleys and out of rivers, sometimes carrying a low layer of fog with it, and is often referred to as 'drainage'.

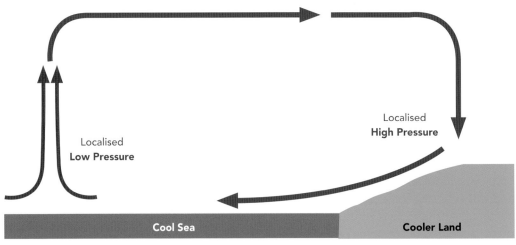

Land breeze at night

PREDICTING GUSTS

Gusts are generally caused by parcels of air above the boundary layer, which are travelling at the geostrophic wind velocity, being entrained into the boundary layer randomly.

They keep their momentum from the geostrophic wind and, if they reach the surface, we feel them as gusts.

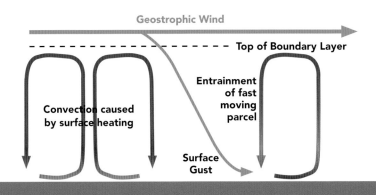

The entrainment of a geostrophic wind air parcel to become a surface gust

Looking at wind forecasts just above the boundary layer gives a good idea of the gusts, and the 925hPa level (700-800m up) is useful for this and easily available as GRIB data.

These two charts show this, with 12 hours difference taking the wind from 24 gusting 31kts (fresh, but still OK for spinnakers given the right equipment and crew) to 26 gusting 43kts (almost certainly not OK for spinnakers!).

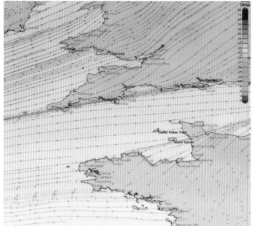 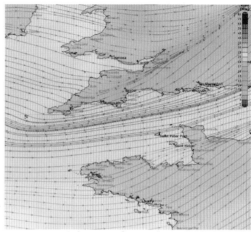

| 0600: 24kts at surface, 31kts at 925hPa | 1800: 26kts at surface, 43kts at 925hPa |

Surface wind streamlines and 925hPa wind speed (shading) 12 hours apart in the English Channel: ahead of what looks like a front coming in (note the veering wind at the 1800 plot) the surface wind is only a little stronger, but it's now gusting to 43kts, Beaufort Force 9

One thing to note – the 925hPa wind usually comes from the right of the surface wind in the Northern Hemisphere, and to the left in the Southern. However, by the time the parcels of fast moving air make it to the surface the chaos of the boundary layer will mean that the gusts are almost always evenly distributed either side of the mean surface wind direction.

RADIATION (LAND) FOG

What you need for radiation (land) fog to develop is an area of semi-enclosed water (for example, a harbour or estuary), and not much gradient wind (for example, if a high pressure system is sitting overhead).

During the day, the air heats up over the sea, and more water evaporates into the air.

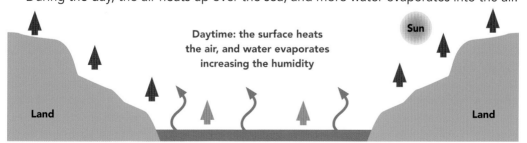

Daytime: the surface heats the air, and water evaporates increasing the humidity

Sun

Land

Land

During the day moisture evaporates into the warming air

As soon as the Sun goes down the air cools, and the water vapour condenses as fog. As the air itself cools it becomes denser and collects in low lying areas, in this case the harbour or estuary, and spills out up to two or three miles from land as the land breeze gently takes it offshore.

When the Sun rises, the air heats up, the moisture again evaporates, and the fog will clear – this is what is meant by the Sun 'burning off' the fog.

So, if at breakfast there is no visibility and little wind, then by about 1100 the fog should have gone and sailing will be possible (depending on the wind). Also, if you can safely navigate your way to open water away from the land, you should have good visibility when you get there.

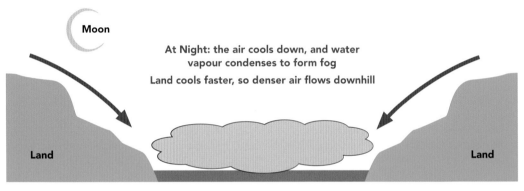

Moon

At Night: the air cools down, and water vapour condenses to form fog

Land cools faster, so denser air flows downhill

Land   Land

At night it condenses again, rolling downhill with the cooler air to form radiation fog

ADVECTION (SEA) FOG

This is caused by relatively warm wet air blowing over cold water: the cold sea surface cools the surface air, causing the water vapour in the air to condense as fog.

This occurs mostly in the spring, when water temperature is coldest after winter and the Tropical Maritime air masses are being brought in from warmer latitudes. This fog is more difficult to shift. An increase in wind speed just brings in more water vapour, and sea fog will still be there up to about a Force 7.

Because new water vapour is being brought in constantly, the Sun cannot heat the air up sufficiently. The only way for sea fog to dissipate is for another air mass, either a Polar Maritime (cold and relatively dry) or a Continental (dry and warm) air mass to come in. This requires a change in the wind direction.

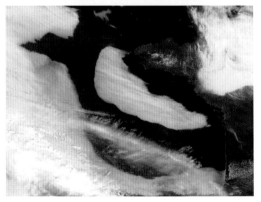

Advection fog in the Bay of Biscay (Image courtesy of University of Dundee Archive Services)

The advection fog shown above is an excellent example of this, showing advection fog being blown to the west away from the coast of Biscay. In the north west corner, the shape of the Brittany coastline can be seen in the edge of the fog bank, and (totally unrelated) there is an algae bloom off the Cornish peninsula.

So, if the conditions in the morning are a steady onshore wind with thick fog, then sailing is probably not going to happen that day unless the wind direction changes significantly.

Interestingly, advection fog can occur over land if the surface temperature is cold enough. January 2010 saw the UK completely covered in snow and this meant that if a southwesterly wind blew then the conditions for advection fog were satisfied (relatively warm and wet air passing over a relatively cold surface) and there were many outbreaks of sea fog – on land as can be seen in the photo below.

The UK snowbound in 2010 creating the opportunity for sea fog on land if a southwesterly wind blew (Image courtesy of University of Dundee Archive Services)

6
TOPOGRAPHIC EFFECTS

So far, we've looked at the big picture of low pressure systems, high pressure systems, Jet Streams, the boundary layer and so on – however, we're most interested in what's going on around us. This chapter deals with topographic effects, the way the land shapes the wind and weather.

BUYS-BALLOT'S LAW & THE EFFECT OF CHANGING THE SURFACE FRICTION OVER LAND & SEA

Buys-Ballot, a Dutch scientist, worked out that if you stand with your back to the wind in the Northern Hemisphere the centre of the low pressure is to your left and in the Southern Hemisphere the centre of the low would be to your right. While this does not seem particularly earth-shattering, it's very useful to help determine what happens to the wind direction as the surface friction changes when wind goes from sea to land or the other way around.

As seems logical, there is more surface friction over land than over sea. This means that wind will slow down over land and speed up over water. The Coriolis Effect depends on the speed, so if the air parcel slows down when it moves from sea to land with an onshore wind, it will fall in faster towards the centre of the low – to the left

in the Northern Hemisphere, to the right in the Southern.

In the Northern Hemisphere, the changing wind direction towards the low over land will cause the wind to back as it moves over land, and veer as it comes off the land on to the water. Conversely in the

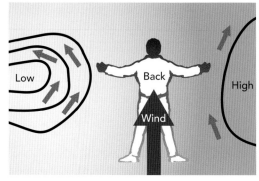

Buys Ballot's Law – Northern Hemisphere

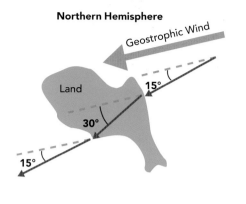

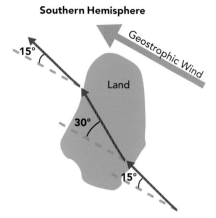

The effect of changing surface friction in the Northern (left) and Southern (right) Hemispheres

Southern Hemisphere the opposite occurs – the wind veers to the right as it slows down over land, and backs to the left again as it accelerates, passing off the land over the water.

BEING HEADED OR LIFTED BESIDE A WINDWARD SHORE

Depending on which tack you're on, it will pay you to go closer in or further off the shore, if an offshore breeze is blowing (this means the shore is a windward shore). The veering as it speeds up doesn't happen immediately, there is a zone of acceleration which depends on the type of land the wind is coming off (cliff heights, long beaches, etc.).

In the Northern Hemisphere the wind veers as it blows offshore and you will be lifted going offshore on starboard tack, and headed if going offshore on port, and it is the other way around in the Southern Hemisphere.

The amount of this direction shift depends on the type of surface of the land – a built up area will give more friction, open grasslands less, and the more surface friction there is over land the more the direction change will be over water.

The distance offshore that this bending happens in depends very much on the temperatures of the land and sea relative to the air. In general, the warmer the surface the more vertical mixing occurs and the sooner offshore it happens. This can be within 1 kilometre of the shore on a summer's day with warm land and sea, and up to 5km on a winter's day with not much heat around.

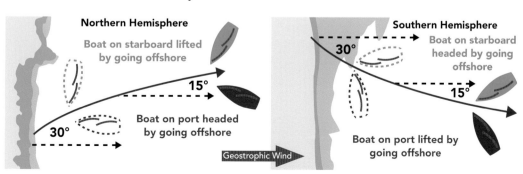

The effect of being inshore and offshore with an offshore breeze

CONVERGENCE & DIVERGENCE

Sailing up a reasonably wide channel (for example, the English Channel, the Skagerrak or Bass Strait), the wind on the side closest to the low pressure system will be slowed down along the coast and fall in towards the centre of the low – this will diverge away from the main flow and thus give less wind near the coast.

On the opposite side the wind along the coast will also slow down, but this causes it to move over the water slightly, causing convergence and therefore stronger winds along the coast.

This doesn't occur just in a channel – if you're sailing with the wind parallel to the coast the same thing occurs.

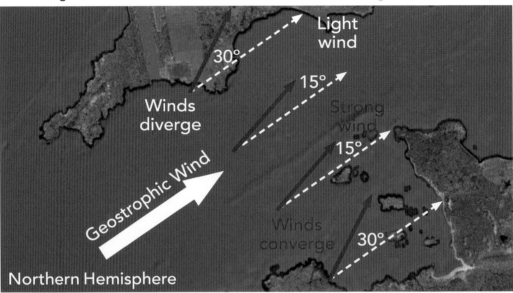

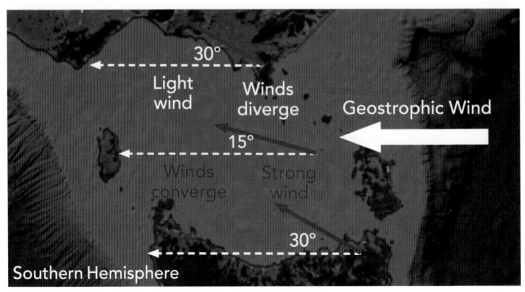

Convergence and divergence in the Northern (top) and Southern (bottom) Hemispheres

ACCELERATION ZONES & HEADLANDS

Acceleration zones occur where the wind is constricted in some way by the local topography, for example, around headlands and in between islands. The zones are usually visible in the day by the change in the surface texture of the water – often referred to as 'wind lines' – as the wind speeds up over that part of the sea. The Canaries are an excellent example to illustrate this (see overleaf).

The Canaries themselves are high volcanic mountains with impressive wind shadows – up to 25 miles to leeward of Gran Canaria, 15 miles to leeward of Isla de Tenerife and 30 miles leeward of Isla de la Palma. They also have significant wind acceleration zones, caused by the displacement of wind along and in between the islands. The air is constricted which causes acceleration, as the only way to get an increased volume of air through the same gap is for it to speed up. The acceleration zones also exist alongside the calm zones in the lee of the islands, and it is easy to stray from one to the other.

A good way to predict where you'll get lees and where you'll get acceleration zones is to look at the prevailing wind direction and actually draw the lines around the land on the chart (electronically or on paper).

This will give you a good idea of the wind lines, which is very useful at night when you can't see them.

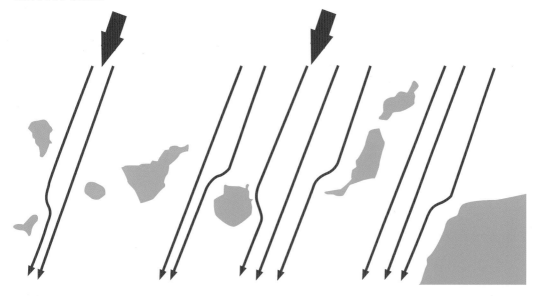

Examples of acceleration zones through the Canaries with a northeast wind, shown by the greater density of wind streamlines

The same thing happens around headlands too, not just through squeezed gaps. Portland Bill in the UK and Cape Byron, the easternmost point of Australia are examples where the wind can be significantly stronger close inshore. Both of these examples also have strong water movement past them, which needs to be considered with wind acceleration when deciding whether to go inshore or stay out.

KATABATIC WINDS

If an area of high ground has had settled weather for a week or so, the air mass on top of it will be cold. If a weak offshore gradient wind arrives, this air mass is pushed over the edge and will sink rapidly down the slope – if you happen to be a couple of miles offshore the wind can increase from the gentle breeze that pushed the air off the top to about 60 knots as the cold air mass builds momentum.

A good example of this are the Bora winds coming from the north or northeast across the northern Adriatic off the Karst and Dinaric Alps. In general, the higher the plateau the faster the wind and the larger the plateau the longer it will last, because there's more of it. A more violent example are the katabatic winds of the Antarctic, especially where they are funnelled by valleys.

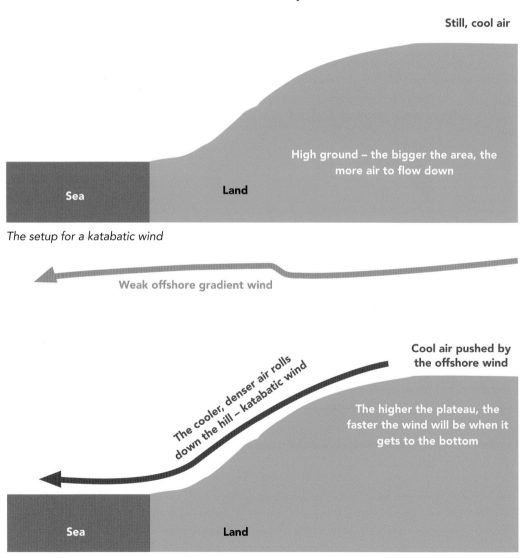

Still, cool air

High ground – the bigger the area, the more air to flow down

Sea

Land

The setup for a katabatic wind

Weak offshore gradient wind

The cooler, denser air rolls down the hill – katabatic wind

Cool air pushed by the offshore wind

The higher the plateau, the faster the wind will be when it gets to the bottom

Sea

Land

The cool air pushed over the edge by a light offshore gradient

Even with a reef in, the boat is still pushed right over by the onset of katabatic wind

FOEHN (OR CHINOOK) WINDS

If a wind blows over an open plain or an ocean and is then forced upwards by a mountain range, it is subject to orographic lifting. As it rises, the air will cool and water vapour will condense to clouds and fall as rain.

The process of condensation also makes the air a little warmer, so on the leeward side of the high ground the descending wind is much drier and also warmer. The dry air is a Foehn wind and means that fewer clouds develop, so the downwind side also tends to be sunnier, which in turn makes it warmer again.

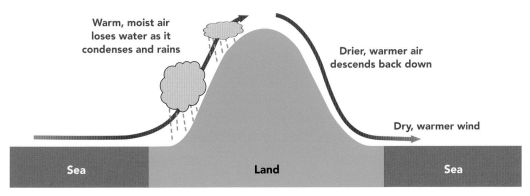

Warm, moist air loses water as it condenses and rains

Drier, warmer air descends back down

Dry, warmer wind

Sea   **Land**   **Sea**

Foehn wind mechanism

7

TROPICAL WEATHER

When we are talking about tropical weather, the first thing to do is to come up with a definition of what constitutes 'the Tropics'.

Navigationally, it's easy; the Tropics are defined as being between the Tropic of Cancer at 23° 26'N and the Tropic of Capricorn at 23° 26'S.

Meteorologically, this doesn't work though.

A better way of looking at it is to think of the energy arriving from the Sun. The amount of heat supplied to any point by the Sun depends fundamentally on its latitude, and the amount of heat re-radiated by that point by its surface temperature. As the

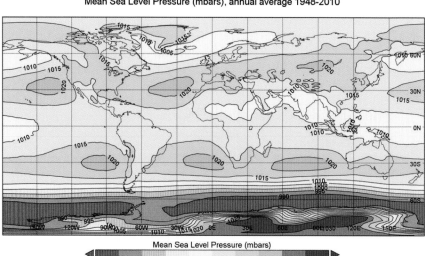

Mean Sea Level Pressure (mbars), annual average 1948-2010

The Tropics: meteorologically in between the mid-ocean highs and the Equator

latitudes around the Equator receive more heat than the ones nearer the Poles this leads to an imbalance, and also to a useful and practical meteorological definition of the Tropics.

From a sailor's perspective, the Tropics can be defined as the part of the Earth's surface which receives more solar radiation than it radiates back out. The tropical weather systems, together with the ocean currents, act to transport this heat away from the Tropics towards the Poles – if this did not happen then the Tropics would keep getting hotter, and the Poles would keep getting colder.

So, this gives us a basic meteorological definition of the Tropics – the regions between the sub-tropical ocean highs and the Equator, approximately 30°N to 30°S where the main driver of the circulation is the Hadley Cell.

Looking at the North Atlantic Hadley Cell in more detail it can be seen that the excess heat of the Tropics is taken away vertically by rising convection in the Inter Tropical Convergence Zone (ITCZ), and then taken polewards by the upper level winds. By about 30°N the air no longer gets enough heat from the surface and cools more, becoming denser and subsiding towards the surface to form the North Atlantic High. This descending dry air forms an inversion layer stopping the surface heating and convection from rising too far, which effectively puts a lid on the Trade Wind clouds. The surface Trade Winds themselves blow in towards the ITCZ picking up moisture along the way. There are two main transports happening at the ITCZ – heat going up vertically, and moisture coming in horizontally.

One important point is that the air here is generally much warmer than in the mid-latitudes and can therefore absorb more water vapour. This means that if the relative humidity is 90% in the Tropics there is significantly more water in a given volume of air than if it were a relative humidity of 90% in Europe or New Zealand. The net result of this is that, when it rains, it really rains, and there is far more moisture and energy in tropical weather than in mid-latitude weather.

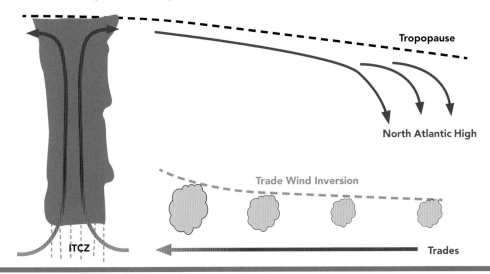

The North Atlantic Hadley Cell

THE TRADE WINDS

The surface Trade Winds are driven by the pressure difference between the mid-ocean high and the ITCZ (upper chart), with the Coriolis Effect bending them to the right (lower chart).

As you might expect, the bigger the pressure difference between the high and the ITCZ, the stronger the Trades are on any given day. This brings in the first big conceptual difference for predicting tropical weather – the ITCZ stays at pretty much the same pressure, it doesn't vary a lot at all. Therefore the strength of the mid-ocean high is what drives the strength of the Trades, and the higher the pressure, the stronger the wind, which if you've done a lot of middle latitude sailing takes

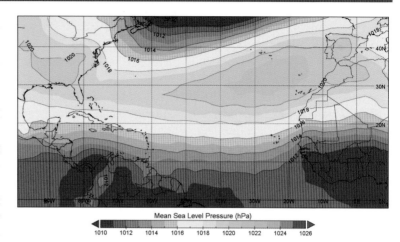

Mean sea level pressure for Dec-Feb,1949-2010: the North Atlantic High is centred just south of the Azores and it extends a ridge all the way across to Florida; the pressure gradient between this and the low pressure band that is the ITCZ on and just north of the Equator drives the Trade Winds

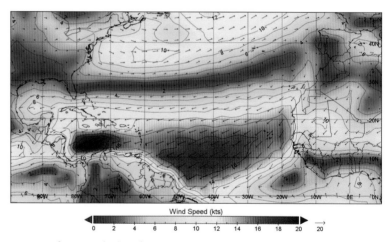

Mean surface winds (kts) for Dec-Feb, 1949-2010 showing how the Trade winds blow consistently all the way across the tropical Atlantic; the ridge from the centre of the high just south of the Azores all the way to Florida is characterised by light and variable winds

a little while to get used to. Traditionally in the North Atlantic the Trade Winds are usually picked up south of the Canary Islands at about 25°N, and there's a grain of truth in the easy way to navigate to the Caribbean – 'go south till the butter melts and then turn right'. However, average conditions are just that, average, and are made up of many different scenarios.

An important point is that the Tropics to a large extent just have one air mass – Tropical Maritime – and so the whole concept of weather fronts just doesn't exist. Because the Hadley Cell and therefore the

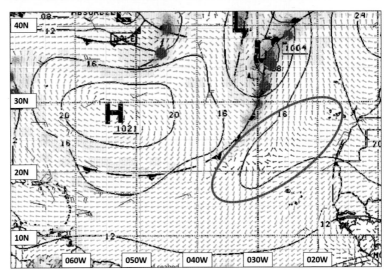

Trades are strongest in winter, though, there are fairly regular occurrences of deep low pressure systems polewards of the high dragging cold fronts over tropical regions.

The Trades are generally quite steady, but if a deep low moves towards the Equator this can both push the high down too and trail a front down to the Tropics, both of which will severely affect the Trade Winds.

The North Atlantic has a low at 36°N 029°W, and trails a front down to the southwest, effectively splitting the high in two; ahead of this the Trades are disrupted (red outline) – this has GRIB data for wind (arrows) and rainfall (blue shading) overlaid on to a NOAA synoptic chart

The chart above shows how the low at 36°N 029°W trails a front down to the southwest and this effectively splits the high. The Trades are knocked right down ahead of this front, with light and variable wind there. As an aside, this illustrates the use of precipitation data (the blue shading) to show fronts up if you don't have access to synoptic charts at sea.

THE INTER-TROPICAL CONVERGENCE ZONE (THE ITCZ)

This is also known as the Doldrums and has an undeserved reputation as being a windless hole where nothing happens. Sailing through it is actually really hard work, as the wind comes from all directions and can vary greatly in strength, which can lead to expensive mistakes with lightweight sailcloth.

As the name suggests, this is the zone where the two Hadley Cells meet, so at the surface this is where the northeast Trades converge with the southeast Trades. In the North Atlantic the ITCZ varies from just north of the Equator in December to about 10°N in July and August.

The position of the ITCZ depends on the area of highest sea surface temperature, and this broadly speaking follows the Sun north and south. Surrounding land masses and deep water currents also play a part in this. In the North Atlantic the ITCZ tends to be widest near the West African coast, and it can be seen overleaf that, as it is further to the north, the southeast Trades are bent to the right by the Coriolis Effect as they cross the Equator, ending up as south or southwest winds by the time they converge into the ITCZ.

As you approach the ITCZ a sign that you are no more than a day away from it is the sight of very high wispy clouds going the opposite direction to the surface winds you are sailing in. This is rather disconcerting but it is the upper part of the Hadley Cell taking the last bit of moisture out and means that you are nearly at the ITCZ itself.

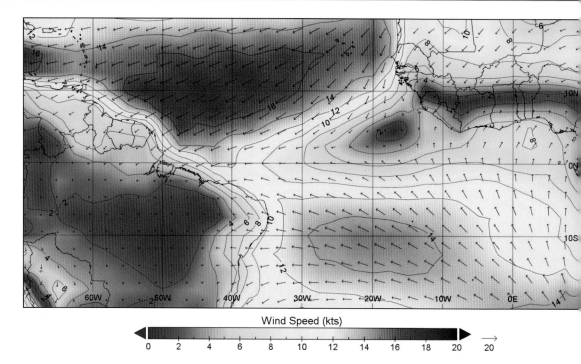

Wind Speed (kts)

Mast height winds (kts) in the North Atlantic for December, 1948-2010 with the northeast Trades meeting the southeast Trades at the ITCZ; note that the southeast Trades from the South Atlantic veer right as they cross the Equator due to the Coriolis Effect changing sides

The ITCZ is by no means a uniform wall of convection and therefore cloud. These two examples, a week apart in August 2010, show very different convection patterns. A common aiming point if you're heading from Europe to South America is to cross the ITCZ at around 025-028°W. The earlier date here has the ITCZ about a degree wide, so 60 miles. The second date has it about 4 degrees wide there, so 240 miles – that's a lot more very variable wind to deal with.

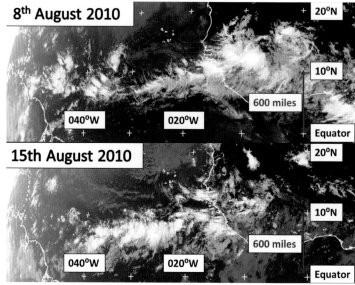

Thermal infra-red satellite images from 8 (top) & 15 (bottom) August 2010: at 27°W the ITCZ cloud band is only 1° wide, so 60 miles, on the 8th but a week later it's 3-4° wide, so 180-240 miles; this will make a big difference to how long it takes to transit (Images courtesy of Dundee Archive Services)

These two images also show how the ITCZ moves around, and if you don't have access to the internet at sea the best information on this comes from the automated weather messages on the GMDSS system which arrive on INMARSAT-C data receivers, as shown below:

ITCZ AT 08N020W, 09N030W, 07N040W AND 06N050W WITH 3/4 DEGREES WIDE WITH LIGHT/MOD ISOL SHWRS IN THE WHOLE BAND.

You may not have the choice, but the ideal scenario is to cross the ITCZ when it is going the opposite direction to you, i.e. north if you're south bound or south if you're north bound. A good level of vigilance is required going through it, as there is no prevailing wind and everything is squall driven, so what is your leeward side one minute may be the windward side the next.

DIURNAL VARIATION

As you get to within about 30° of the Equator the barometer will start to exhibit a twice daily rise and fall on top of the changes due to the low and high pressure systems. These changes (small at first but can be up to ±2hPa) are masked by the general weather in the higher latitudes, but the more settled pressure regime of the Tropics allows them to be seen. The times of local maximum pressure are usually 1000 and 2200 local time, and minimums are at 1600 and 0400 local time, and the relevant pilot book will give the amount of the correction. It's very important to record the actual pressure in your logbook and note the correction as a remark – don't just write down the corrected value. This allows you to see if the diurnal variation disappears, which is one of the signs of an approaching Tropical Revolving Storm.

The timing of this is the clue to its cause – it happens 2 hours ahead of local noon. The Sun's radiation is short wave, and as such not absorbed much at all by the troposphere. However, the thermosphere, the very outer layer of the atmosphere, is warmed up by the Sun and so expands. The expanding air cannot go to the east, as that has already been warmed, and so goes west. This means that there is physically a little more air above the ground just ahead of the Sun, which means there is a slightly higher pressure (no more than 4hPa in 1,000hPa) ahead of the Sun, at 1000 local time. This sets up a wave which has two wavelengths around the globe, hence another maximum 12 hours later (or earlier, depending on how you look at it) with minimums in between.

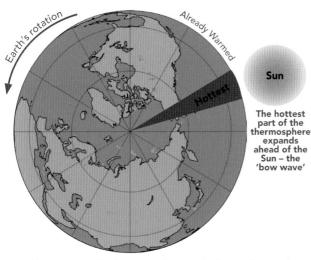

Diurnal variation, looking at the Earth from above the North Pole

TROPICAL WAVES

These are a North Atlantic phenomenon which are also known as African Easterly Waves. Some of them do continue through the Caribbean and into the tropical East Pacific, and, in the summer, these can trigger Tropical Revolving Storms throughout the tropical North Atlantic and Eastern Pacific.

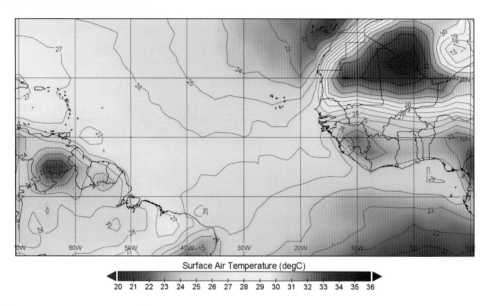

Surface air temperature (°C) for Jul-Oct 1948-2010: the Sahara is much warmer than the tropical Atlantic to the south

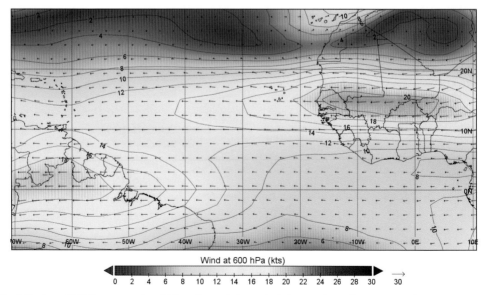

Wind (kts) at 600hPa, around 4,200m, for Jul-Oct 1948-2010: the African Easterly Jet is not very strong but carries all the way across to the Caribbean

They are a direct result of the Sahara Desert being consistently significantly hotter than the seas around it. This causes a large temperature gradient with the sea at the Equator being cooler than the Sahara. This temperature difference gives us a mid-atmosphere Jet Stream, called the African Easterly Jet (AEJ), and because the temperature is higher in the north the AEJ goes from east to west.

The AEJ causes mid-level disturbances every two to three days, very much like eddies on the edge of a fast-moving stream of water, and these are Tropical Waves. They are effectively troughs moving to the west at about 15 to 25 knots, with the wind backing then veering as they go over, and more convection therefore more squall activity, increased wind and gusts with more rainfall. They are normally not dangerous in themselves and are actually a good opportunity to replenish water tanks, but can be the triggers for hurricanes depending on the time of year. In September, these waves are strongest and approximately 40% of them go on to develop into named storms, i.e. winds greater than 34 knots.

The example shown below passed over the rowing boat Monkey Fist Adventure en route to Antigua from the Cape Verdes.

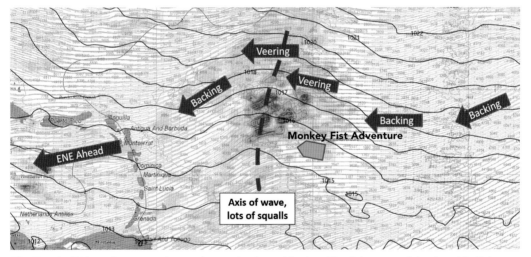

The Tropical Wave that passed over the rowing boat Monkey Fist Adventure (blue boat) in February 2020; note the isobar shape, the squall activity around the wave's axis (blue shading) and the wind backing ahead of it, then veering behind before finally backing to the Trades again

MONSOONS

The name derives from the Arabic for 'season' and refers to seasonal weather conditions that are caused by large areas of land either heating up or cooling down. The most commonly encountered ones at sea are the Indian Monsoon, the East Asian Monsoon and the Northern Australian, or Austral, Monsoon.

The Indian Monsoon is a summer monsoon and hits every year at about the first week in July and is caused by the heat of the Arabian and Asian deserts causing a heat low. This brings in air cyclonically around it from the Indian Ocean, and when this wet southwesterly wind hits the Indian subcontinent it rains – a lot.

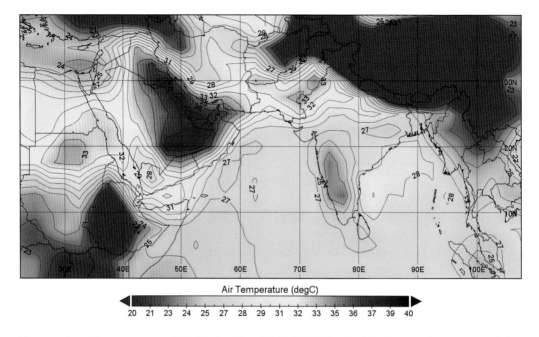

Air Temperature (degC)

20 21 23 24 25 27 28 29 31 32 33 35 36 37 39 40

Mean surface air temperature (°C) for Jun-Aug 1948-2010: the Arabian Peninsula is extremely hot, and this causes a semi-permanent heat low to sit above it

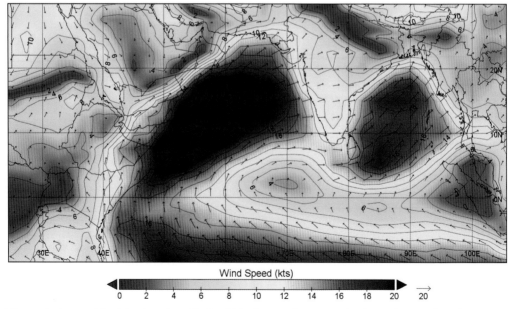

Wind Speed (kts)

0 2 4 6 8 10 12 14 16 18 20 20

Mean wind speed (kts) for Jun-Aug 1948-2010: the southeast Trades from the South Indian Ocean come across the Equator and are then accelerated by the cyclonic circulation around the hot Arabian Peninsula, taking a strong and very humid flow onto the Indian subcontinent

The East Asian Monsoon is a winter monsoon, and a high is formed by the temperature dropping dramatically over the high East Asian land mass – note the large change from on land to over sea. This gives rise to anticyclonic circulation, and a NE monsoon down the east coast of China towards Singapore.

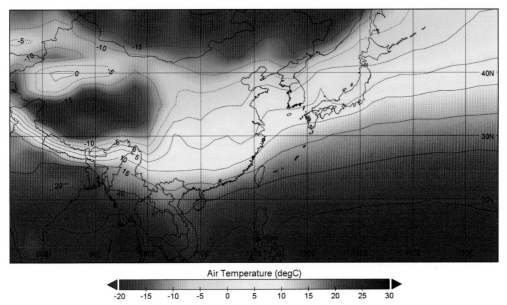

Air Temperature (degC)

Mean surface air temperature (°C) for Dec-Feb 1949-2010: the interior of Asia is very cold, causing a semi-permanent high pressure system and encouraging anticyclonic flow around it

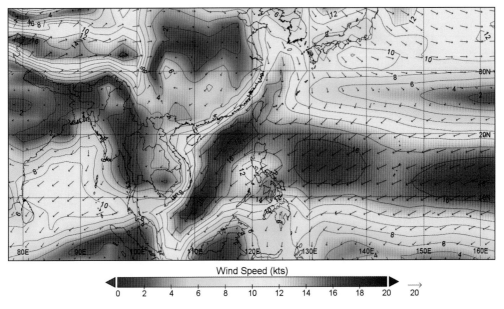

Wind Speed (kts)

Mean surface winds (kts) for Dec-Feb 1949-2010: the anticyclonic flow around the cold interior high is steadiest as the northeast flow past Taiwan and through the South China Sea

SQUALLS

Squalls are self-contained convective systems, often confined to less than a mile or so in diameter, but they can occur in clusters of several hundred miles in spread. They are common in the Tropics, and the warmer the water is, the more active they will be.

The first thing is to work out where they will move with respect to you, and during the day the Mark 1 eyeball is the best method to use. Simply treat any worrying squall cloud as if it was an approaching ship – if it is on a reasonably steady bearing and doesn't seem to be going to port or starboard of you, then it will pass over you. Likewise, if it seems to be opening its bearing to pass ahead or astern of you then that is what it will do.

At night a good radar watch should be kept, so make sure, if you have it, that you look at your set every quarter of an hour or so. A visual watch is still effective at night of course, as an approaching squall will start to block out the otherwise bright stars. If you do pick one up on radar, put an Electronic Bearing Line (EBL) on it and monitor it – if the squall marches straight down the line it is going to pass over you. At this point you may want to change course, reduce sail or both!

Let's look at a simple squall first:

- Warm air will rise to start with and, as it is over the ocean, it will be moist.
- As this rises it cools, and the water will start to condense to form clouds.
- The cloud droplets will increase in size until their weight exceeds the upward force of the updraft and they will fall as rain.
- As the rising air reaches the top of the squall cloud it will have been cooled more than the surrounding air due to the energy taken out by the water condensing and so this air will fall down the outside of the cloud and some inside it as cold downdrafts (which is what you often feel just before a squall actually passes over you).
- Also, the raindrops themselves will drag air down with them, causing further downdrafts inside the cloud.
- This eventually counteracts the updraft of warm air, and the squall just seems to rain itself out, with the cloud base getting higher and higher until it disappears.

Squalls developing at dawn in the tropical Northern Atlantic

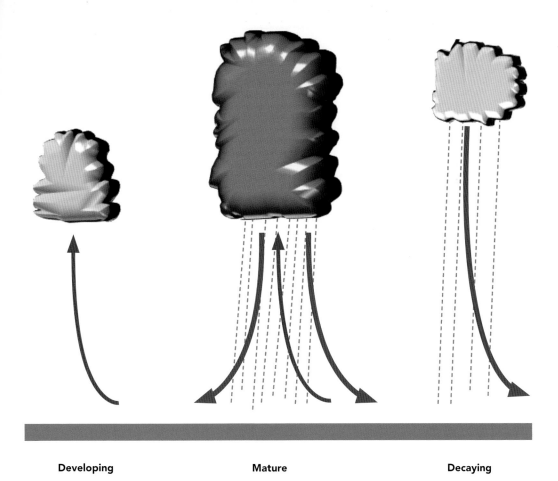

| Developing | Mature | Decaying |

The development and self-immolation of a simple squall

However, if there is a steady wind blowing this will give wind shear, the phenomenon whereby surface friction slows the surface wind down and it increases in speed with altitude until the steady gradient wind speed is reached.

This is the situation which will give rise to self-sustaining squalls:

- The wind shear makes the whole convective system lean over, which then makes the precipitation and therefore the cold downdrafts fall away from the warm thermal updrafts.
- As these cold downdrafts hit the surface, they spread out in all directions,

including against the regional wind.

- As the cold downdrafts are denser than the surface air they will actually force this warmer air to rise (shown by the diagonal purple line in diagram overleaf) and this process will carry on at night like a miniature front – the system is effectively generating its own lifting mechanism.
- Also, if the velocity of the downdraft as it spreads out over the surface is the same as that of the regional wind, the system will effectively stay at the same place – and if that's directly above your boat, you have no choice but to bob around until it slowly moves off.

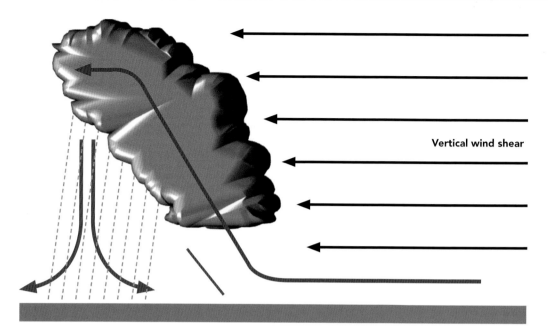

Vertical wind shear

A self-sustaining squall

The squall will also have a localised effect on the general gradient wind:

- If the squall is directly coming at you, the gusts will add to the gradient wind, increasing the wind you feel.
- If it passes ahead of you, the gusts will act against the gradient wind, decreasing or sometimes even reversing it.
- If the squall passes to the side of you then, depending on the spatial relationship, it will back or veer the wind – basically the local wind always blows away from the base of the cloud.

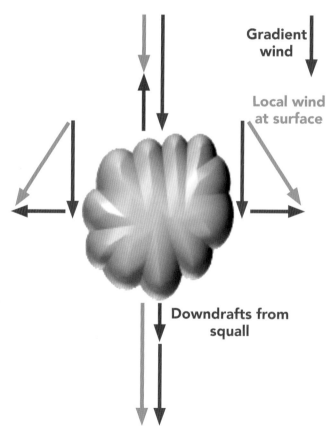

Gradient wind

Local wind at surface

Downdrafts from squall

The effect of squall gusts on local wind

If you're sailing **upwind** and a squall comes towards you then it all depends whether the squall is going over, behind (your windward side) or ahead (down your leeward side) of you:

■ If it passes behind you then you should get lifted, with stronger wind, until the squall is past.

■ If it goes ahead of you then you'll be headed as it approaches, so you can tack and take the lift on the opposite tack before tacking back again when you're subsequently headed as the wind reverts to normal.

■ If it goes overhead, then hang on to the mainsheet and enjoy the gust!

While going **downwind**, if the cloud comes on your windward side, then you end up being lifted as it goes past, while if it passes down the leeward side you'll be headed.

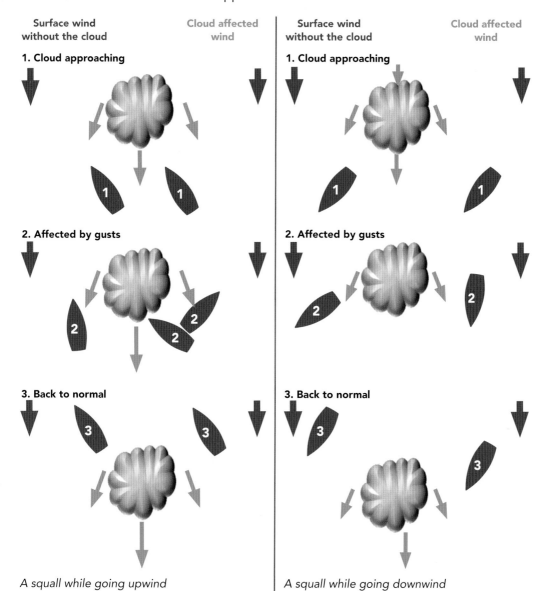

| Surface wind without the cloud | Cloud affected wind | Surface wind without the cloud | Cloud affected wind |

1. Cloud approaching

2. Affected by gusts

3. Back to normal

A squall while going upwind

A squall while going downwind

8

TROPICAL REVOLVING STORMS

These deep low pressure systems with sustained winds greater than or equal to Force 12 are called different things in different parts of the world:

- In the North Atlantic and East Pacific they are **hurricanes**
- In the West Pacific and the Southern and Northern Indian Oceans they are **cyclones**
- Over Eastern Asia they are **typhoons**

North Atlantic Tropical Revolving Storms (TRS) are categorised by their sustained winds on the Saffir-Simpson Scale:

- Tropical Depression (TD): Up to 34kts
- Tropical Storm (TS): 35-63kts
- Category 1 hurricane: 64-82kts
- Category 2 hurricane: 83-95kts
- Category 3 hurricane: 96-113kts
- Category 4 hurricane: 114-135kts
- Category 5 hurricane: >135kts

CONDITIONS FOR TRS DEVELOPMENT

They start off as low pressure systems and, as they are in the Tropics, there are no fronts involved as the air mass is the same throughout.

There are six basic conditions for a TRS to start:

1. **MOISTURE**. Dry mid-tropospheric layers can snuff a TRS out.
2. **ROTATION**. More than 5° away from the Equator to have enough Coriolis Effect.
3. **LITTLE VERTICAL SHEAR**. This is the difference in wind speed from surface to the top of the troposphere. If there is a large vertical shear, then vertical air movement is inhibited.
4. **UPPER LEVEL DIVERGENCE** to aid the vertical air movement.
5. **A TRIGGER** of some sort – something like a Tropical Wave with increased convection.
6. **SEA SURFACE TEMPERATURES ABOVE 26°C TO MORE THAN 60m DEPTH**. This provides the ongoing source of heat and moisture for the TRS even with a large sea state, bringing cooler water up to the surface

The first five of these can happen at any

time of year, but the sixth one, the sea surface temperature, needs some consistent warming and so the hurricane seasons in various parts of the world are when the sea is at its warmest. This explains why the North Atlantic Hurricane Season is approximately June to November, with early season hurricanes tending to start in the warmer Western Atlantic or the Caribbean waters, and why the Southern Pacific one is approximately November through to April.

STRUCTURE OF A TRS

These can be thought of as all of the Tropics in one system, with all that energy packed into a much smaller area. There is strong convergence at the surface, vertical movement through the middle, and divergence at altitude.

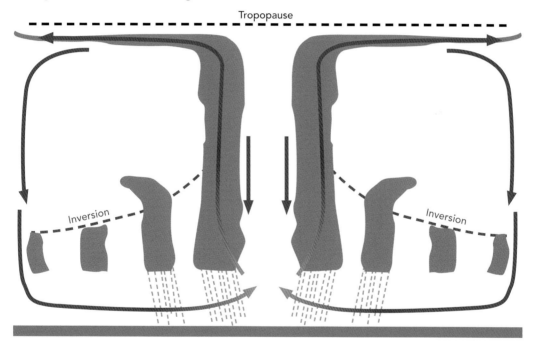

Schematic of a TRS

Satellite radar and visual images of Hurricane Isabel in September 2003 show how this works in reality, with the inner cloud walls showing up very well on radar, indicating much rainfall there. Another important point demonstrated is the lack of any weather fronts, as it is all the same air mass.

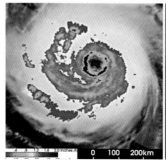

Radar (left) and visual (right) images of Hurricane Isabel, September 2003

SIGNS OF AN APPROACHING TRS

These are well forecast, so if you have any communication with the outside world then you will have decent warning of them. However, both Sod and Murphy are sailors, so if your communication systems go down at just the wrong time then there are several things you can observe and measure from your yacht.

Wind: TRS's vary in size, but a 'typical' one will have Tropical Storm (34 knots plus) winds out at about 150 miles from the centre. A large one will have these winds at 300 miles out. In the North Atlantic the wind is usually east / northeast, and this will back as the TRS approaches.

In the Southern Hemisphere the Trades are usually east / southeast, and will veer as the TRS approaches.

Swell: TRS generate a long swell from the direction of their centres (at least where they were at the time). For example, the usual swell period in the North Atlantic is 6 to 8 seconds; if this increases to 9 to 12 seconds then a TRS probably exists, and if it's 12 to 15 seconds it definitely does.

Clouds: The TRS throws out moisture and wind at the upper levels, and these will be visible as high level cirrus at between 300 and 600 miles. As the TRS gets closer this cloud cover will thicken and lower, until heavy cloud walls of cumulonimbus clouds and strong showers and squalls appear about 200 to 400 miles from the eye of the storm.

Barometric Pressure: The centre of a TRS can have remarkably low pressures (e.g. 888hPa for Hurricane Gilbert in September 1988), and so any signs of pressure consistently dropping below the tropical and sub-tropical norm (about 1,012 to 1,020hPa) should make you take note. The TRS itself is not a smooth steady system, and the vast amounts of air coming into, going up and coming out of a TRS can cause minor fluctuations in pressure – known as a pumping action. This usually has the effect of masking the usual diurnal variation and causing it to disappear.

THE SURFACE STRUCTURE OF A TRS

The whole TRS usually (there are exceptions!) moves at about 15 to 25 knots, and this leads to the designation of two halves – the 'dangerous semicircle' on the polewards side of the track, and the 'navigable semicircle' on the equatorwards side (north and south sides in the Northern Hemisphere, the other way round in the Southern).

The two sides are given these designations as the wind you see on the surface is the vector sum of the wind speed around the centre and the forward speed of the TRS itself. The examples opposite gives sustained winds of 100 knots in the dangerous and 70 knots in the navigable semicircles – it is, just, possible to make tea in 70 knots, but nowhere near in 100 knots.

A further problem is that the TRS is more likely to recurve to the north and northeast in the Northern Hemisphere, south and southeast in the Southern and so, if you are polewards of its track, it could end up following you.

To work out which semicircle you are in the path of use Buys-Ballot's law, which states that if you stand with your back to the wind in the Northern Hemisphere the centre of the low will be to your left, and if in the Southern Hemisphere to your right.

Because of surface friction the wind will angle in towards the low by about 15°, so once you are standing with your back to the wind, move the relevant arm (left in the north, right in the south) forward 15° and take that bearing – that is where the TRS centre is.

In the Northern Hemisphere, if this bearing veers towards the south, then the TRS centre is moving south of you and you're in the path of the dangerous semicircle; if it backs and moves towards the north then you're in the path of the navigable semicircle. Conversely in the Southern Hemisphere if it backs towards the north, the dangerous semicircle is on the way, and if it veers towards the south, the navigable side has you in its sights.

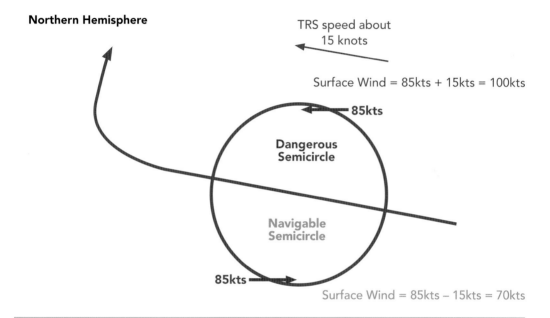

Northern Hemisphere

TRS speed about 15 knots

Surface Wind = 85kts + 15kts = 100kts

85kts

Dangerous Semicircle

Navigable Semicircle

85kts

Surface Wind = 85kts – 15kts = 70kts

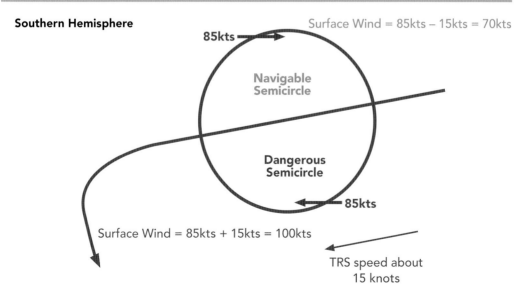

Southern Hemisphere

Surface Wind = 85kts – 15kts = 70kts

85kts

Navigable Semicircle

Dangerous Semicircle

85kts

Surface Wind = 85kts + 15kts = 100kts

TRS speed about 15 knots

A surface schematic of Northern (top) and Southern (bottom) Hemisphere Tropical Revolving Storms

RECOMMENDED ACTIONS TO ESCAPE AN ONCOMING TRS

This depends which semicircle you're trying to avoid, and both require tea!

If you find yourself in the dangerous semicircle then you have two options:

1. You can try to cross the front of the storm and make it in to the navigable semicircle

2. Or you go as close to the wind as you can on starboard tack (port in the Southern Hemisphere) and follow it round as you get away from the track of the eye

The first of these, getting across the front, is often not possible on a sailboat, as you have to increase speed considerably – think of it as a different, but equally fraught, version of deciding whether you can safely get across the bows of an oncoming container ship.

The second option is most likely going to be your only one, but the big danger here is that the TRS recurves and just keeps following you.

If you are in the navigable semicircle, then still stay on starboard tack (port in the Southern Hemisphere) but sail on a broad reach to take you out of the path of the eye. It'll still be dangerous, and the storm may decide to follow you, but it's a lot better than being on the other side of the storm.

Northern Hemisphere

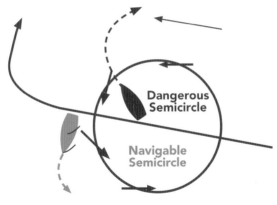

Southern Hemisphere

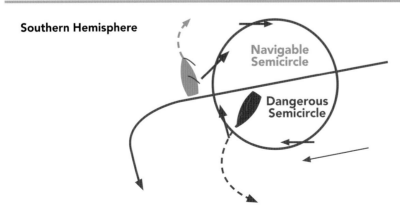

Avoidance tracks for an oncoming TRS

9

CLOUDS

Clouds are more than just decoration; they give us an insight into what is happening and what is about to happen. They are made of countless billions of tiny water droplets or ice crystals, and are surprisingly heavy – a cumulus cloud with a volume of 1 cubic kilometre weighs approximately half a million kilograms, for example.

So, what keeps them up there? The answer to that is rising air – each individual droplet has a very small mass compared to its surface area, so the upward flow of rising air will easily keep it there. This means that the cloud patterns give you an idea of the three-dimensional pattern of the air, and of how the wind you get at surface will feel.

If you look at the site of the wonderful Cloud Appreciation Society you'll find a huge array of different cloud types and classifications but, from a sailor's point of view, there are 5 words with which you can record clouds in the logbook and make up the types that are of immediate use for your forecasting at sea.

- **Cirrus**: A high level tuft or filament
- **Cumulus**: The classic fluffy 'Mr Man Cloud' usually deeper than they are wide
- **Stratus**: Layered cloud
- **Nimbus**: Rain bearing cloud (usually a darker more ominous grey)
- **Alto**: Mid-level clouds, usually from around 2 to 7km up

With these five words you can describe all the main cloud types and, more importantly, get an understanding of what they're telling you.

Roll cloud downwind from the mountains in Palma

HIGH PRESSURE SYSTEM CLOUDS

High pressure systems are by their nature fairly stable and are often associated with reasonably steady winds. However, the clouds give us an idea of the nature of these winds.

CUMULUS

The two images show the fair weather cumulus clouds at Weymouth on the south coast of the UK in an offshore northeasterly wind on a warm summer's day with a high off to the west. The morning shot (left) taken at 1010 has some clouds, but by 1308 (right), once the land has warmed up, there are many more. This is why the distribution of fair weather cumulus is such a useful indicator as to how shifty & puffy your wind is.

Cumulus clouds at Weymouth, UK, in an offshore northeasterly: the morning shot (1010, left) shows small puffs of cloud, the afternoon one (1308, right) many more of them

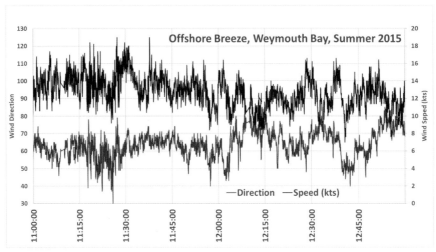

The wind trace that day, showing wind direction (degrees magnetic, red) and wind speed (kts, blue) from on the water reading every 2s (with permission from the British Sailing Team)

The section on squalls (p78) describes the wind around squall clouds, and the same thing happens with their smaller fair-weather cousins. In Weymouth that day, the wind changed accordingly – in the morning it was fairly steady but after noon there was much more of a difference between gust and lull wind speeds and the left / right shifts went from ±10° to ±20°.

Another common sighting of cumulus clouds in a high pressure system is as sea breeze clouds (see p57), and here they are an excellent indicator of the state of the cell – if they're growing, your sea breeze will strengthen, and as they top out and then start to shrink, your sea breeze will ease.

Cumulus clouds building inland over Guanabara Bay – good signs for an afternoon sea breeze

STRATUS

These tend to be low quite thin layers in a high pressure system and can even end up as fog if they are low enough.

Broken stratus clouds over Carrick Roads, UK, with radiation fog, effectively sea-level stratus cloud, filling the harbour beneath it

LOW PRESSURE SYSTEM CLOUDS

Ahead of the warm front or after the cold front in the relatively cold and dry air masses either side of the warm sector, you'll find scattered fair-weather cumulus clouds, much as in the winds around a high. These are generally fair-weather clouds and are mostly white. The colour of a cloud, particularly a low one, depends on the droplet size – larger droplets absorb more light than small ones, so a cloud that's white has smaller droplets which require a weaker updraft to hold them up.

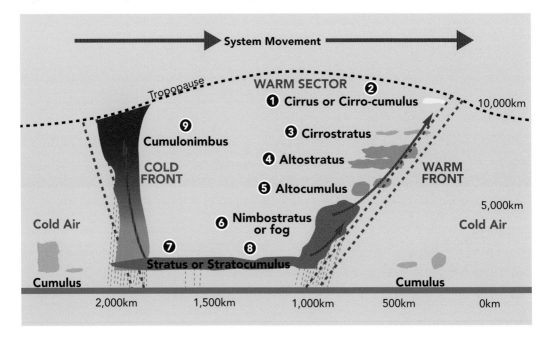

1. CIRRUS
First you will see these high wispy clouds that look like strands of hair (which is what cirrus means in Latin). If you're expecting a warm front, this is usually the first sign.

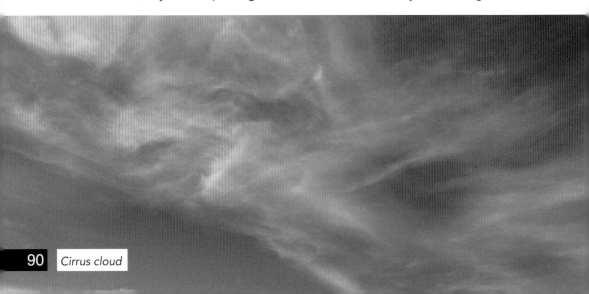

Cirrus cloud

2. CIRROCUMULUS

Sometimes with the cirrus clouds you will see cirrocumulus. These form the classic mackerel sky ahead of a depression, and usually one with quite a lot of moisture in it to have that much at the very top of the troposphere. This is why these are often seen as harbingers of stronger weather. Sometimes however, they are just clouds, and beautiful ones at that.

Cirrocumulus cloud

3. CIRROSTRATUS

As the front approaches, the cirrus clouds will start to join together to form a more uniform covering. It's still high up and thin though, so won't block out much of the Sun's light.

4. ALTOSTRATUS

The cloud continues to thicken and lower as the front approaches, and altostratus is usually low enough to contain water droplets as well as ice crystals, so usually start to look darker and you may get some light rain (or snow in winter).

Cirrostratus cloud

Altostratus cloud above cumulus cloud

5. ALTOCUMULUS

Still in the mid-levels now altocumulus tends to be more lumpy and bubbly than the stratus clouds, hence the name. They are generally above the surface thermals so are more an indicator of an approaching front than of the pattern of the surface wind.

Altocumulus cloud

6. NIMBOSTRATUS

This arrives just before and with the warm front itself – a lower, darker thicker layer cloud, and, as the 'nimbo' suggests, usually rain bearing. If it's down at the surface, it will also be fog. There are often brighter patches in it, but it's a good cloud to view while holding a mug of something warm and sustaining.

Nimbostratus cloud

7. STRATUS

Once the front is through then you're into the warm sector of the low, where the weather is usually steadier. Stratus cloud is a low layer of cloud, usually fairly uniform from below. However, when seen from above there are usually distinct bands of deeper and thinner cloud, as shown in the photo opposite. This was taken above Palma in spring, and while the stratus cloud was featureless from below the breeze had bands of stronger wind in it – and looking at the shape of the clouds above explains why. Stratus clouds often have a bandy wind underneath them, with large and slow moving patches of cloud-driven wind.

The top of a stratus cloud over Cadiz in the spring, showing the bands of deeper and shallower cloud which will give rise to bands of stronger & lighter wind beneath them

8. STRATOCUMULUS

If the warm sector is more active, around a deeper low, it may have stratocumulus; a layer of broken cumulus clouds instead of stratus clouds in between the fronts. These are far less uniform than the stratus cloud, so the breeze will be less steady underneath them – as ever the shape of the low clouds indicates the shape of the surface wind.

Stratocumulus cloud

9. CUMULONIMBUS

These are the kings and queens of the cloud kingdom – huge, deep, dark heat engines rising from just above the surface to potentially the tropopause. They are usually the darkest of clouds, with the biggest droplets in them, and often contain hailstones too as the droplets are carried above the freezing level. Underneath these clouds we get the strongest squalls and heaviest rain, with a good possibility of thunder and lightning too.

Cumulonimbus cloud

CREDITS

CREDITS FOR PHOTOGRAPHS, DIAGRAMS, GRAPHS, CHARTS & DATA NOT GENERATED BY SIMON ROWELL

PHOTOGRAPHS & DIAGRAMS

Kevin Law: p5; British Sailing Team: p6 & 88 (bottom); Matthew Dickens: p7; Dom Tidey: p28; alybaba / shutterstock.com: p48 (top); Fernhurst Books Limited: 62; Frank Everaert: p67, 78; NASA Earth Observatory: p83 (bottom); Alberto Masnovo / shutterstock.com: p93 (bottom); Alex Stemmer / shutterstock.com: back cover.

WEATHER DATA, GRAPHS & CHARTS

Dundee Satellite: p45 (satellite), 46 (bottom), 60 (bottom), 61, 72 (bottom) – Images courtesy of University of Dundee Archive Services: used with permission.

ECMWF: Data: p10 (bottom), 17, 18:
1. Copyright © 2020 European Centre for Medium-Range Weather Forecasts (ECMWF).
2. Source www.ecmwf.int
3. Licence Statement: This data is published under a Creative Commons Attribution 4.0 International (CC BY 4.0). https://creativecommons.org/licenses/by/4.0/

Expedition.com: Drawing: p25, 71, 75: used with permission.

Met Office: p22 (top), 38 (top), 40 (bottom), 41 (left), 45 (charts), 47 (bottom): (contain public sector information licensed under the Open Government Licence v1.0.).

NOAA/NWS: p23 (bottom), 24, 26, 46 (top), 52, 71
NOAA/NWS: Data: p16, 20 (bottom), 25, 29, 32, 33, 34, 36, 50 (bottom), 51, 54, 59 (top), 68, 70, 72 (top), 74, 75, 76, 77
This data is in the public domain.

South African Weather Service: p38 (bottom) – Historical Synoptic Charts 2017, October (accessed 21 October 2017), 53 – Historical Synoptic Charts 2019, October / November (accessed 31 October, 1 November, 2 November 2019), http://www.weathersa.co.za/home/historicalsynoptic: used with permission.

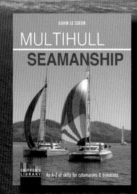

FERNHURST

B O O K S

We hope you enjoyed this book

If you did, **please post a review on Amazon**

Discover more books on

SAILING · RACING · CRUISING · MOTOR BOATING

SWIMMING · DIVING · SURFING

CANOEING · KAYAKING · FISHING

View our full range of titles at **www.fernhurstbooks.com**

Sign up to receive details of new books & exclusive special offers at

www.fernhurstbooks.com/register

Get to know us more on **social media**